Ex Líbris

Alpines
for your garden

Alan Bloom

Published 1981 by Floraprint U.S.A., Chicago, IL.
North American Edition © Floraprint U.S.A., 1981
First published 1980 by Editions Floraisse,
Antony, France. © Editions Floraisse.

ISBN 0-938804-01-4
Library of Congress 80-70904

Alan Bloom, author of many books on hardy perennials and alpine plants, has been involved in raising and growing these subjects for over fifty years. His long experience covers both plant production and practical gardening. As a specialist his experience covered large scale production, and as a plant lover, of growing plants for their own sakes—evidence of which shows up in *Perennials for your Garden*. His methods of growing alpines for display are sometimes unconventional, but are always effective as the photographs in this book taken at Bressingham more than prove.

The Publisher wishes to express his appreciation in being allowed to take photographs at the following gardens:

Bressingham Gardens, Norfolk.

R.F. Britten, Esq., Chelsworth, Suffolk.

Froyle Mill, Hampshire. (Mr. and Mrs. Taylor-Smith)

Messrs. R.C. Gibbs and O. Griffiths, Chelsworth, Suffolk.

Harlow Car Gardens, Harrogate. (The Superintendent)

Little Park, Flowton, Suffolk. (R.A. Brooks, Esq.)

Mr. and Mrs. M. Newman, Oliver's Battery, Winchester, Hampshire.

Royal Horticultural Society, Wisley. (The Director)

Savill Gardens, Windsor Great Park. (Crown Estate Commissioners)

M. Sawyer, Esq., Ipswich, Suffolk.

M. Smith, Esq., Ipswich, Suffolk.

Snipelands, Pebmarsh, Essex. (Mrs. U.M. Nott)

University Botanic Garden, Cambridge. (The Director)

Unusual Plants, Elmstead Market, Essex. (Mrs. Beth Chatto)

Derek Fell, one of America's leading national garden writers, has edited Alan Bloom's work to help make it applicable for the United States. A frequent contributor to *Horticulture* and other national publications, he has authored several garden books of his own. In editing Alan Bloom's work, which is based largely on British conditions, Fell attempted to preserve as much of Bloom's original writing, including his variety recommendations, which are becoming increasingly available in the United States. Garden centers now handle a number of alpines, but the more exotic varieties will need to be attained through mailorder sources.

The appeal of alpines is not only their infinite variety and sometimes dainty, fairyland appearance, but the fact that most are high altitude plants used to cool temperatures. They make an excellent hobby for greenhouse gardeners because they require no more than frost exclusion—thus saving on heating bills.

Gypsophila 'Dorothy Teacher', *pink flowered, grows in the foreground. Behind, Helichrysum alveolatum is a foil for the brighter colors of an orange helianthemum, yellow Genista sagittalis and blue Veronica prostrata.*

Introduction

In using the word 'alpine' for the plants of garden value it does not mean they all originate from the Alps. Nor does it mean that all come from various other mountainous regions. It is merely a convenient word for lack of a better term by which to describe the vast group of low dwarf or slow growing plants which can be effectively used in gardens. The term 'rockery' or 'rock garden' plants is inadequate because very few kinds in this group need rocks between which to grow. The majority are very adaptable, both as regards soil and climate, but this book deals only with those which are both winter-hardy and perennial. Those of merely annual duration, along with many dwarf bulbous subjects are excluded because they are seldom compatible with the wide and more interesting range of perennials. These are also more satisfying to grow, and my general list of recommendations is made up almost entirely of kinds which are reliable in a wide variety of situations. This must be emphasized. An artificially made rockery or rock garden is not the only place, nor necessarily the best place in which to grow alpines. One main objective of this book is to describe the various ways in which alpine plants can be grown to good effect, and with the minimum of trouble and after-care.

Historical background

The cultivation of alpine plants is a relatively new practice, arising chiefly from the explorations of the past two hundred years. During that time the explorers, who were often botanists, brought back, mainly to Europe, large collections of newly discovered plants from the wild. Among them were small growing kinds as well as tall, and, of course, trees and shrubs. The latter were easier to place in botanic and other gardens, but the small growing kinds needed a place to themselves, where they would not be overshadowed or invaded. It was, therefore, a natural outcome to choose a site where they could be fully seen and appreciated. Because many were found where rock formations abounded, or were from high-altitudes, the introduction of rocks appeared as an enhancement to the nineteenth century gardeners. Hence the term 'rockery' or 'rock garden' came into use, along with 'alpines' for the whole range of plants, since the European Alps were the first to be explored. Very few true rock gardens existed before 1900. It is true that by that time the so-called 'rockery' was becoming a popular feature, but it was often ridiculously exaggerated and quite out of keeping both aesthetically and for the welfare of all but the more robust kinds. It consisted usually of a mound of earth, often in an obscure or shady situation, on which were dotted lumps of stone without the least regard for beauty or fitness. Between the stones, were spaces called 'pockets' for the plants, but so often the choicer kinds died in such harsh, unnatural conditions. And the mound itself was often difficult to weed or water, so that only the more rampant, weedy kinds survived, to take possession.

The 'rockery cult' still survives in cases where garden owners know no better—sometimes using even lumps of concrete as a substitute for rocks, but those who build rock gardens with rocks, to imitate a piece of mountain scenery, have not always succeeded. The placing of rocks to advantage both for the plants and as a garden feature can easily result in failure or an offensive eyesore, and it must be said, that in many gardens away from rocky or hilly areas, an imitation piece of mountain scenery is out of place. There are other, better means of growing alpine plants in gardens where flatness or formality are predominant, and these are described later on in the book.

Categories of alpine plants

As a generalization, it is safe to say that the most successful gardens are those where the plants grown are naturally suited or adaptable to the prevailing conditions of soil, situation and climate. This can certainly be applied to the cultivation of alpine plants. Though so many are quite adaptable, it stands to reason that those native to high alpine screes and moraines will need different conditions to those inhabiting woods, or meadows, tundra or sandy banks at low altitudes. The same applies to latitudes, where their long-standing habitat has put limits on the degree of hardiness and moisture requirement.

It follows on evolutionary principles that, in adapting themselves to the prevailing conditions in nature, the habit of growth shows wide variations. The term 'habit' has become accepted for describing the type of growth, and in alpines this falls into several sections. From the highest altitudes and dry rock places, one finds most of those having a slow growth rate, and they are often of low hummock or cushion formation, with minute leaves or rosettes. These are often known as scree plants, needing very little soil, but very good drainage. They are found growing at altitudes well over 3,200 feet where, from October to May, they may be under snow. But during this long period, they remain relatively dry, because little or no moisture soaks down to their roots until the snow begins to melt. Then, as summer comes, one can see the thrilling, almost miraculous sight of flowers peering through the remaining snow. It is the short period of growth, with cold nights, which has made such plants as *Gentiana verna, Soldanella* and many saxifrages so diminutive. They remain so in gardens despite more favorable climatic conditions, even if they may spread more quickly.

In cultivation they are, as might be expected, the most difficult to adapt to garden conditions, needing the gritty soil, but often objecting to both winter wet and summer drought and heat. They are often used to best advantage in stone sinks and troughs, but some are best in what is known as an alpine house, where the glass coverage keeps off winter wet and where moisture requirements in summer can be met.

Because of their special needs, not many scree plants are mentioned in the list of recommendations, but the variety available is so wide that a number of cushion-forming plants which are less fussy is included. Another habit group includes those which have a bushy, semi-shrubby formation. These may be upright or more spreading, evergreen or deciduous, as far as foliage is concerned, but coming from a more or less central root, with life retained above ground over winter, whether or not foliage is lost. They are described as of bushy or trailing habit, and are generally easy to grow. Examples of the erect and bushy type are seen in *Iberis* and *Helianthemum, Gypsophila* and some penstemons of the trailing kinds.

In the wild, most bush-forming alpines are found on hills and mountains bordering on the Mediterranean or in the Near and Middle East. There, summers are hot and dry, but when roots can penetrate deeply or into rock crevices and walls, they can survive. Unlike plants growing in a mild, moist climate, leaves and stems hold very little sap which is often an indication of a low rainfall, for all but a short rainy season. It is then that new growth and flowering takes place. In gardens, this range of plants will often flourish but may need trimming, to remain shapely and neat.

Other groups having growth habits of their own include those of mat-like growth. These (along with carpeters) often root down into the soil as they spread, but with varying rapidity. More often than not, these keep themselves clothed over winter. Some smother themselves with flowers in summer, but others are grown for foliage alone, in silvery hues as well as greens. These have several uses and are among the easiest to grow, including such well-known subjects as *Aubrieta,* alpine phlox and thymes.

One other important type are those which die down in true herbaceous character, to a live, but scarcely visible, rootstock during winter dormancy. They are often found in alpine meadows or anywhere where there is a fair depth of soil. Because of competition with other plants, including grasses, in a natural habitat, they survive by sharing on a compromise existence. This is achieved by evolutionary processes whereby some associate with plants having a different root system. The roots feed at different levels, while growth at and above ground level is more or less shared, often at different heights to obtain necessary air and light. It is interesting to note that there are examples of some plants which will grow better in association with others because this has become a natural feature of adaptation.

They may be clump-forming, which means they expand in size but do not spread by underground shoots. The large genus of *Campanula* includes some with this habit. Others have a fairly rapid spread from below the surface, but summer growth is not retained. Among kinds with this habit of spreading underground are some which can be a nuisance because of invasion into other kinds. Advice is given on how best to avoid harmful competition, and any species with this habit is given in the general descriptive list, as are those of a rampant nature. The distinction here is that rampant means rapid spread above ground, and invasive refers to spread below the surface. There are, of course, some alpines which in habit fall somewhere between two of those loosely defined above. This serves to emphasize the infinite variety in habit of growth, as well as in the range of adaptability and uses to which the plants can be put. In turn, it points to there being alpines suitable for almost any position in a garden. A selection of plants can be made that will grow happily there. But the vast majority of kinds prefer an open, sunny position, well drained but not too deprived of moisture. This means that the most difficult site to clothe with alpines, as with taller herbaceous or border plants, is that of dry shade under trees, where roots starve the soil and where low, overhanging branches keep out sunlight and air circulation.

The first consideration for those wishing to grow alpine plants for beauty's sake, out of interest in the plants themselves, should, therefore, be to decide on a site. If restrictions as to the choice of a site exist, then, whatever is decided, it should be accepted that not only must preparations be made to give the plants the best possible chance, but that the selection of kinds to be grown will be in keeping with the site and their adaptability to it.

Ways and means to grow alpines

In most gardens a site can be found where a pleasing selection of plants can be grown successfully. The ideal, as well as the most common, is an open position, having a fair amount of sunlight. This will enable the widest and most colorful range to be grown, but there comes the need to decide on the means of growing them. Assuming the garden is flat or gently sloping, with no natural rock formation, the decision must be made whether or not to use rocks at all. As a garden feature, a rockery or rock garden clumsily or unskillfully constructed can easily spoil the overall design. It can also prove to be expensive, difficult to maintain, and restrictive as a means of growing plants successfully, if rocks take up too much space and are badly placed. This is not to decry the use of rocks but merely to encourage the garden owner to think carefully before introducing them. Some may feel that it is as much out of keeping to grow alpines without rocks as others would see them as incongruous in a flat, rectangular, suburban garden. It is a matter of personal choice, but one of the most glaring examples I remember seeing was a miniature 10 foot high 'Matterhorn' built by an alpine enthusiast as the focal point of a rock garden, within a garden surrounded by a brick wall. My own belief is, that if one wishes to grow alpines for their own sake, other means exist whereby rocks, if they are used at all, are limited to easing slopes or gently breaking up any tendency to flatness.

There are many variations on this theme of growing plants for beauty's sake without the extravagant use of rocks as a rockery or rock garden. But, because so many kinds are diminutive, it is worth considering a raised bed especially for them, and unless the ground has sufficient natural slope to form a terrace or bank, it involves building a low wall. So does terracing where a slope is already steep enough to allow erosion to take place, or so slight that a bed cannot be raised without one. The alternative to a wall, if there is no objection to bending down to view more closely or tend the lowliest plants is to have a 'walkabout' bed. Such a bed could be raised slightly by using stone or bricks around its perimeter, filling in with a suitable soil mixture for the plants. Access by means of flat stones or bricks on which to tread is an easy matter to arrange.

Terracing, raised beds and 'walkabout' beds are all dealt with separately below, along with rock gardens large or small. Detailed advice is given on preparation, construction and maintenance.

The importance of drainage

The first essential, applicable to all methods is to ensure good drainage, and this is largely dependent on the existing type of soil. In most cases the nature of the topsoil is in turn determined by the subsoil. If it is sand or gravel, the topsoil will be light and drainage no problem. But a heavy topsoil, hard when dry and sticky when

A section spoiled by rather indiscriminate planting. Acaena pulchella (below) is encroaching and would have been better used elsewhere as groundcover. Here and there appear leaves of a variegated hedera (ivy), which is likewise out of place.

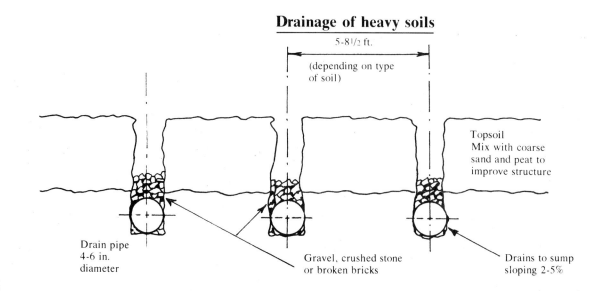

Drainage of heavy soils

5-8½ ft.

(depending on type of soil)

Topsoil
Mix with coarse sand and peat to improve structure

Drain pipe
4-6 in.
diameter

Gravel, crushed stone
or broken bricks

Drains to sump
sloping 2-5%

Terrace wall

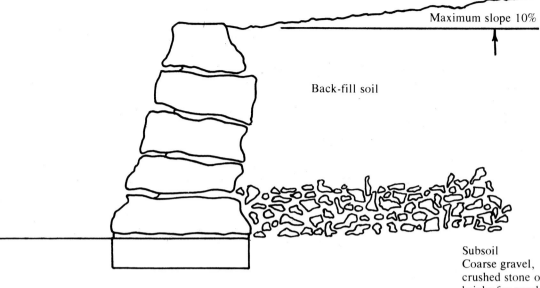

Maximum slope 10%

Back-fill soil

Subsoil
Coarse gravel,
crushed stone or
bricks for good
drainage where subsoil
is heavy clay

wet usually indicates clay as being the subsoil. Clays may vary from sticky marl, to the tough grey-blue or yellowish type, but all are, to some extent, resistent to water and liable to impede drainage if consolidated. To overcome this, one must either import soil of a lighter nature as an overlay of at least 20 in., having first dug and broken up the natural soil, or insert drains. These can be ordinary field drain pipes, baked clay, or perforated plastic laid as a grid 20-24 in. below the surface, with a gentle fall to carry soakage water away. In some gardens such water can be run into a ditch, a pool, or to another part where moisture-loving plants can be grown. An alternative to drain pipes, is to back-fill each narrow trench with a 6-8 in. layer of shingle, broken stone, etc. Having provided drainage, it is still advisable to add a light soil mix containing grit in some form to a depth of at least 10 in. as a growing medium. Soil mixtures for various conditions are given under each heading.

Drainage is especially vital if rocks are to be used where the basic soil is clay. The weight, not only of the rocks themselves, but arising from the effort of placing them in position, tends to ram or consolidate the soil which may then impede natural water percolation.

Treatment of weeds

In all circumstances the need to eradicate pernicious weeds is of vital importance. In this respect, perennial weeds, such as thistles, dandelions, bindweed, chickweed and plantain, to mention some of the worst, must be killed at the outset. Forking out is not always effective and although most weeds can be killed outright by chemicals, expert advice should be taken as to which to use. How and when to apply and how long the chemical will remain toxic in the soil are other considerations. Many a project has been ruined by neglecting the weed factor. Although annual weeds, too, can be a nuisance, they are more easily killed by sprays, by hoeing, or in the case of raised beds, by adding a sterilized soil mix to a sufficient depth above any natural soil, which nearly always holds certain seeds of annual weeds awaiting a chance to germinate.

Raised beds and terraces

A raised bed is expected to appeal most to those with limited garden space. It is to be recommended as the most adaptable for any open situation, and as a means of giving expression to an interest in alpine plants. It is purely a matter of personal choice as to its shape or size—as well as to the extent to which it is raised above the natural level. A decision must also be made whether to provide an island site with all-round access or to place it against an existing wall. In some gardens, where a narrow flower border against a wall has become more of a nuisance than an attraction, a raised bed can make a pleasing and interesting transformation. If, however, the existing wall is that of a house, damp penetration from the bed might be a restrictive factor.

A raised bed can be of any height its owner wishes, but generally a wall of about 24 in. is adequate. The retaining wall should not be of solid concrete or bricks, which would give a harsh appearance, and take years of weathering to soften. Old bricks could be used, as could concrete blocks as a last resort if toned down with a subdued color cement coating. But neither of these can match stone, which gives the most pleasing appearance. One other great advantage of stone is that in using irregular shapes and sizes one can leave niches between them in which plants can grow, rooting through into the soil behind.

A colorful raised border of alpines during May to June, the peak period for display, in which silver-leaved and white-flowered plants break up the predominantly pink and red subjects.

Terrace wall

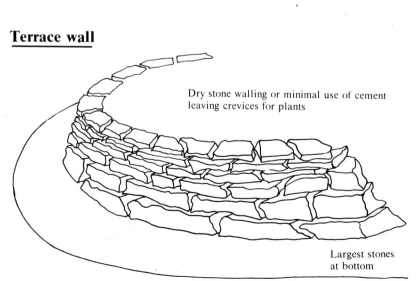

Dry stone walling or minimal use of cement leaving crevices for plants

Largest stones at bottom

Angular rocks or stones are, therefore, best used for effect and will fit better with one another to make cementing virtually unnecessary. Dry stone walling may be thought of as a craft, but given angular stones, it is not beyond an amateur's capability to build a sturdy wall. The vital factor of drainage applies also to walls, whether for a raised bed or terracing. If no outlets are made to allow drainage, the bed will continually be damp and the wall will also be likely to experience damage from freezing and thawing. Outlets should be placed in the lower portion of the wall, where soil pressure is greatest. A low wall of 12 in. or less is not affected, providing a fairly loose soil mix is used in the bed.

One method for a raised bed is to use dry stone walling with a backward slope. Such a slope of about 70-80 degrees adds strength against the pressure of the soil behind and is necessary where the height of the bed, or of a terracing wall, is more than 24 in. In Munich Botanic Garden a raised bed was made with sloping walls to a height 60 in. It is oblong, with all-round access, and having a flat top of 40-60 in. across at eye level. The whole construction is designed to be fully clothed with plants, including the sloping walls. Such a design may not have a wide appeal, and I imagine watering would be a much greater problem than drainage, no matter what permeation quality the subsoil possesses. It is mentioned as an extreme example of how many variations exist on this theme of raised beds, where the interest is centered on alpine plants in all their fascinating variety.

The higher an island bed is raised, within reasonable limits, the greater the variety that can be grown. If it has a sunny side it has also a shady one, in which shade-loving plants can be grown on a north-facing wall. But while access for viewing and tending is easier with an island site, the reach factor should not be overlooked. A high bed should not be so wide as to be beyond one's reach, and so climbing up onto it for maintenance weeding or planting becomes necessary. A low bed of 24 in. or less would not pose any such problem, nor would a backward slope to the wall be necessary other than to resist heaving, caused by freezing and thawing. It is worth mentioning, however, that small or rounded stones and rocks would not be as stable a building material, as larger, angular ones, and any question of back slope or the use of cement to ensure strength and stability would be a matter of discretion.

In recent years, peat blocks have been recommended, though mainly to act as a retaining wall for peat beds. They are not very stable, especially in dry areas, because they tend to shrink and waste away. Although advice is given on peat beds on page 13 they should not be included in the present context covering open positions in which mainly sun-loving plants, most of which are lime-tolerant, are grown.

Terracing slopes

Walls should lean backwards for strength

Natural slope

Level existing topsoil within each terrace and add new soil mixture

This broad sweep of a gentle slope, with few rocks and having slabs for access, is a most attractive and commendable piece of landscaping for alpines. Even the vacant spaces are not out of keeping with a 'natural' formation, though their overall interest would have been increased had they been occupied. Less trouble results, however, from sparse planting than from overcrowding.

Advice on creating an alpine bed by means of terracing is largely covered by that given for island raised beds, or as a one-sided border. It follows, of course, that a two-sided border, regardless of width, is in fact an island bed, and as a strip of no more than 20-24 in. wide it can be very effective. If a gentle slope exists, it could have a low terrace wall on the one side, to make it about equal the level of the other. This is in fact a terrace, and the height of the wall can vary according to the angle of the slope. Slopes of more than 30 degrees should be terraced because most soils erode if some means of containment is not attempted. Terracing can modify the slope of the planting bed to 10 degrees or less, depending on the desire of the gardener. There can, of course, be more than one terrace wall for a steep or continuous slope, designed to grow plants both above and in cracks of the wall itself to give a spectacular effect in spring and summer. One sees vineyards in very hilly countries completely terraced, but in gardens, more steps for full access would be needed. When terracing, care should be taken not only to build walls strong enough

to withstand the pressure of soil they retain, but to conserve the topsoil. When a natural slope exists, the topsoil is seldom deep, and it would be a mistake to use subsoil with which to back-fill. Instead, it should be left virtually intact, except for being cleaned, loosened, and leveled off with imported soil.

'Walkabout' beds

The one other type of bed in which rocks play no ornamental role is the 'walkabout'. This is merely one which is on a fairly natural level, with perhaps only stones, bricks or rocks as a curb round the perimeter. As with a raised bed it can be of any shape or size to fit in with the surroundings. Any stones used within would be merely to break up the flatness, apart from those used as stepping-stones for access. Flatness is not really a problem in any alpine bed where rocks are limited or excluded, because dwarf shrubs of many kinds, especially conifers, will serve to create focal points,

thereby making such a bed interesting. It is always a good idea, however, to place these plants before herbaceous types are added to the bed.

A little elevation for a 'walkabout' bed has two advantages. One is that it calls for the addition of some soil. This can be of a type not only to cover a natural soil which is poor, heavy or otherwise not ideal as a growing medium, but it also greatly reduces the thrust from latent annual weeds. It can also be varied, so that if, for example, the wish is to grow lime-hating kinds, one section of a bed could be filled with a peaty or otherwise lime-free soil. In this event, it would need to be at least 12 in. deep. Some excavation may be needed to achieve it.

For some, the use of rustic wood could be an alternative to bricks or stone to form a curb to a bed with a low elevation. It would, of course, need to be stripped of bark, which may harbor insect pests, slugs or snails as it rotted, and hasten rotting of the timber within. Branches of between 6 in. and 12 in. thickness of a durable hardwood such as oak or hickory would be best. If cut into lengths of two yards and upwards they would hold the soil for sev-

'Walkabout' bed

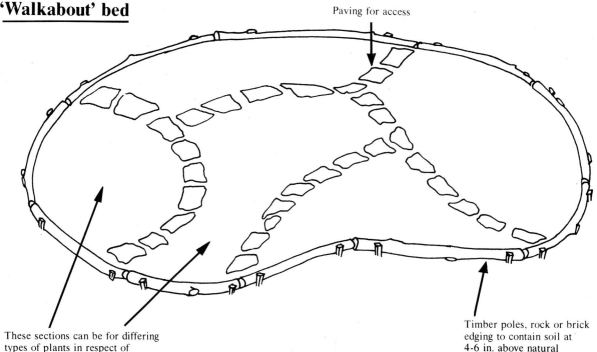

Paving for access

These sections can be for differing types of plants in respect of growth or soil requirements

Timber poles, rock or brick edging to contain soil at 4-6 in. above natural level (optional feature)

eral years. The logs would be laid to conform roughly with the desired shape of the bed. But care would be needed if a second layer were to be used to gain elevation. Nails or wire may be required to hold them in position.

Rock gardens

Finally, so far as especially selected sites for alpines are concerned, advice must be given for those who wish to indulge in a rock garden. They may see no incongruity in using imported rocks in an area far removed, perhaps in distance as well as appearance, from a natural rocky setting. This being the case, rocks can be placed to appear as they would in nature. The effect, if some elementary rules are followed, can be very pleasing. The first of these is to avoid peaks and excessive height above the natural garden level. This is not only for aesthetic reasons, which will be clear enough. A peak or miniature mountain would be prone to drying-out, and even if it became well established with plants, access for maintenance would be difficult. It would be much more in keeping, as well as effective for beauty's sake, to keep the contours low, depending, of course, on how large an area the rock garden is to occupy. The larger the area, especially if a slope already exists, the more imposing a rock formation can be. Again, use large, angular rocks rather than small ones. They will be much more stable.

Assuming that a site is fairly open, has been well prepared for drainage and freed of troublesome weeds, the best plan to follow is that of making tiered outcrops. To some extent this comes back to terracing. Rocks are positioned as if they have always been there, protruding in layers from within a slope. Such outcrops as ledges or terraces need be no more than 20 in. high and at least half of each rock should be buried in the slope. A series of such ledges or outcrops, avoiding regularity, will gain all the height required, and the space they occupy be much less than half. Unless the size of rocks is specified when ordering, a buyer may find some too large to handle alone, for it takes

A limestone rock garden shows how rocks should be placed to give a natural appearance. There has also been a careful siting of plants which, although well established, are not competing harmfully. The vigorous Sedum f. 'Weihenstephaner Gold' (bottom right) is about to affect the choice Geranium cinerium subcaulescens 'Splendens' to the left of it, but, otherwise, there are few criticisms that could be made.

Rock garden building

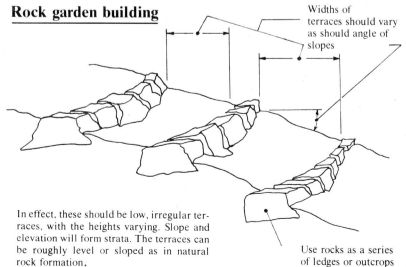

Widths of terraces should vary as should angle of slopes

In effect, these should be low, irregular terraces, with the heights varying. Slope and elevation will form strata. The terraces can be roughly level or sloped as in natural rock formation.

Use rocks as a series of ledges or outcrops

less than a cubic yard of some kinds to weigh a ton. No matter what size rock one uses, the soil beneath and round its base should be well consolidated. This applies especially for dry walling.

Suitable rock, such as sandstone or limestone, is expensive depending somewhat on distance. It is also heavy and a ten ton load will not make a large rock garden. Hence another reason to be sparing with it, using it not primarily as the principal feature but as a means of enhancing the display of plants growing on different levels. As for walling, angular pieces are best. They will fit more closely together to form a ledge or outcrop of a much more natural appearance than will rounded boulders. If angular and roughly oblong, they should be placed with the thicker side down. These rocks should not be stuck up on edge like huge teeth or gravestones above soil level. The effect of this would be offensive to any discerning person. A rock garden should always be built into a slope if one exists. In the absence of a significant slope, it would be best sited against a background of evergreens or a shrubbery, but not so close that it could suffer from the penetration of their roots. It should never be placed to come within reach of the roots of trees, or under overhanging tree branches. The evergreen background would offset any harshness, but, if it is accepted that a rock garden should be of low contour in a generally flat surrounding, an island formation would be much less incongruous. Any incongruity is lessened by constructing a rock garden with the principal aim of growing a collection of plants which is given priority for space. Therefore, the more subdued the prominence of rocks, the more space there will be for plants.

Flat rock slabs make the best pathways beside or within a rock garden or 'walkabout' bed. These flat pieces need not be closely fitted if one wishes to grow a selection of plants in the spaces between them. The soil beneath should, however, have a high percentage of sand, because the plant roots would be hindered in a close-packed soil. Apart from this, the paving will settle down best in a loose mixture, but if raised above garden or base level, it will need a curb to hold loose soil in around the edges.

Soil mixtures and percolation

Additional soil will invariably be required for any of the constructions suggested. If procured from a reliable firm familiar with the type of soil in which alpines grow best, it will be initially expensive but may well prove cheapest in the long run. For those willing and able to procure and mix the three principal ingredients, savings can be made with no great effort. Peat, sand and loam are the main ingredients. Of the three, most vital is a weed-free, loamy soil. It is safe to mix 50 percent soil, with equal proportions of sand and peat. Inorganic or organic fertilizer, containing both phosphates and potash, at the rate of about 1 lb. to a cubic yard, should be added to the mix.

This additional soil mixture should be used as a surface layer and, if sterilized, should be weed-free for a year or two. Weeds are, however, likely to appear from drifting wind or be carried in when flowers are seeded, even if the natural soil is deeply covered by sterilized soil. But if unusual weeds are not allowed to grow and seed again, and perennial weeds dealt with on sight, one can keep abreast and prevent them from becoming a problem for the future. The amount and type of sand to be added should vary according to the nature of the soil, whether this comes from the garden or is imported from outside. If already stony or gravelly, then the sand can be reduced. If clay or other soil type with a low content of sand or stones, then it needs the addition, both of sand and compost to assist moisture percolation and drainage. The tendency of a stoneless, clayey soil, even if it contains fine sand, is to pan down when wet. Overconsolidation, means poor drainage in a wet period and hardness when dry. Both are liable to inhibit a good root system in plants and may well lead to winter losses. Plants native to fairly high altitudes or where snow often persists until well into spring are mostly found growing in stony soil. Melting snow runs off or sinks in. Warmth then promotes rapid resurgence, followed quickly by flowering. It is not until fading and seeding takes place that the soil beneath becomes drier.

This is nature's way and where alpine plants are grown at low altitudes or where snow is absent or irregular, winter drainage is the most vital factor for survival. Additional moisture during droughty summers is easy to apply, and in free-draining soil, does not have a panning effect. The best additives for heavy or clay soils, are those of a porous nature. Flinty gravel is not so good as crushed rock, bricks or even clinker ash in this respect.

Apart from being mindful of the possible lime content of these materials, as of the basic soil, if lime-hating plants are to be grown, a simple test for the correct porosity can be made. Make a little heap of three or four shovels full then pat the top to make it slightly dished. Take a can of water and pour some gently on the saucer-shaped top. If the water runs through into the soil rather than form a puddle or run off, the mixture will be satisfactory to use. An initial test before mixing would be to try balling up a handful of the basic soil when damp. If it refuses to consolidate, or easily crumbles, there will be little need for an opening additive.

Different types of soil mixture

Soil mixtures can, of course, be varied according to the type of plants one wishes to grow. In a garden with more than 6.5 lime content (this figure being roughly neutral), a section of a rock garden or bed will grow lime-hating plants if desired. A depth of 12-16 in. of lime-free soil, or as a peat bed, can quite easily be contrived. A section for scree plants, most of which are lime-tolerant, should have a similar depth of soil in which rock chippings, broken bricks, etc. make up about half the total bulk. Such a bed should be well elevated, but not allowed to become scorched and dried out. One way of reducing this risk is to spread fine stone chippings $1-1\frac{1}{2}$ in. or so thick over the whole area after planting. Very small gravel, mostly known as pea-gravel, will serve the same purpose and can be used as an overall covering where any alpines are grown. It helps to keep annual weeds from seeding and the soil better aerated because rain or irrigation on some soils leaves a harmful crust as the surface dries. Some alpines prefer poor to rich soil—stony rather than one containing humus, and it is surprising to see some growing in the wild where their roots get all they need by foraging in crevices of a rock-face. Others are happy in what appears to be sand or rock rubble, the latter being in fact the make-up of screes—the debris of eroded cliffs or outcrops. In gardens, this can be imitated quite satisfactorily with broken stone, brick, sandy gravel and ashes of a clinkery type, which feel somewhat sharp if squeezed in the hand. Such plants as the very interesting and varied houseleeks *(Sempervivum)* and several silver-leaved carpeters, grow best in these otherwise fairly arid mixtures, needing very little moisture.

Peat beds

A little more needs to be said on peat beds, which, because they are an easy, inexpensive way of growing a wide variety of plants, are becoming increasingly popular. Firstly, it is advisable to use specially cut turfs for walling. These are larger than ordinary building bricks in size and will make a more durable wall than turfs cut for fuel. They should also contain heather or other roots which hold the peat together for a year or two. Such blocks are taken from the upper layers in a natural peat bed being dug for sale. If the blocks are on the small side, or are inclined to break up with handling, it will be asking for trouble to use them as one would a single width in brick. They tend to shrink when becoming dry and walls should be two turfs wide in addition to the practice of overlapping joints as with ordinary brickwork. Where more than two layers of blocks are needed to gain height, place every third, fourth or fifth block at right angles, bedding it in to the back-fill of loose peat mixture. In addition, provide a little back slope to the wall, where the required height is more than 16-20 in.

Another and even safer precaution is to gain height by terracing with peat blocks leaving planting space at the foot of each. By this means, an informal appearance is more easily attained than by having a higher single wall. Leave a level bed on top. Peat beds should never be placed in full sun. So many peat-lovers like some shade, but with peat holding up to eight times its own weight in water when soaked, it follows, that if allowed to dry out, it becomes sterile

Alpines here are used in frontal groups with taller perennials behind as background. This is a good example of the wider adaptability of alpines and it is worth noting that the owner has used upright growing plants, among the dwarfs, to break up any flatness in design.

Peat beds are not practical for most U.S. gardeners. Most use of peat is limited to making soil supplements and for keeping floral arrangements fresh. Although some peat is being burned as fuel, it is primarily for private consumption. No industry is producing peat bricks for fuel purposes. Therefore, if a gardener is near a peat bog, and wishes to fashion a peat bed, he will probably need to cut these bricks himself.

and plants will suffer. When really dry, peat is slow to take up moisture again for water will run off rather than soak in. The best sitings for peat beds are on the north side of a house or wall, or wherever trees cast some shade during the day, without being so close that trouble from drip or root penetration from below may occur.

Peat needs only sand and fertilizer or a little soil by way of additive, to reduce what might be termed as fluffiness. Because its texture is so light, any planting surface should be level or nearly so. To repair natural shrinkage and wastage, an annual top dressing of a fertilized peat mixture is necessary in spring or autumn.

Other uses for alpines

As dwarf hardy perennials, many kinds usually considered as purely alpine or rock garden plants are well adapted to grow in positions fronting taller subjects. Many gardens have a border of perennials, whether of the conventional one-sided type with a backing, or the more modern and effective, less troublesome island bed. Both should be planned with the tallest plants at the rear of the formal one-sided type or on the center parts of the latter. Heights are graded down to the dwarfest kinds at the front. It is there that a variety of alpines can play their part, adding greatly to diversity and interest.

It will be obvious that a selection for frontal border groups should exclude the low carpeting or trailing types, as well as the slow growing, hummock-forming. But there are many in the range which are mainly erect growing about 6-8 in. in height, which are fully adaptable. They include free growing selected kinds of *Achillea, Armeria, Aster, Campanula, Dianthus, Geranium, Helianthemum, Iris, Potentilla, Primula, Ranunculus, Scabiosa, Sedum, Sisyrinchium, Veronica* and *Viola.* In some, slow growth would call for several of a kind to make groups for comparable effect with the taller growing subjects behind. Otherwise, they would enhance and add variety and interest to them with no additional trouble.

Path edging

Some alpines have real value as edging plants beside a path, especially where the latter is of a hard material such as gravel or paving. If, in one or both sides, there are perennials, annuals or shrubs, a 'live' edging can be planted of either all one subject or in variety. Evergreen trouble-free kinds would be preferable to those having no greenery above ground in winter. Outstanding for such a purpose are *Armeria maritima* in variety, *Campanula muralis, Dianthus,* the primrose varieties of *Primula, Scabiosa graminifolia, Achillea tomentosa,* violas and a few others. They would need no attention for a few years, and then only replanting to reduce unwanted spread. All are worthwhile both for flower and foliage. Some, such as *Epimedium,* would do well along a mainly shady walk. Where used as an edging beside grass paths, possible competition from overhang should be considered—and difficulty when mowing the grass. Bricks or stone between plants and path would avoid this.

Border edging

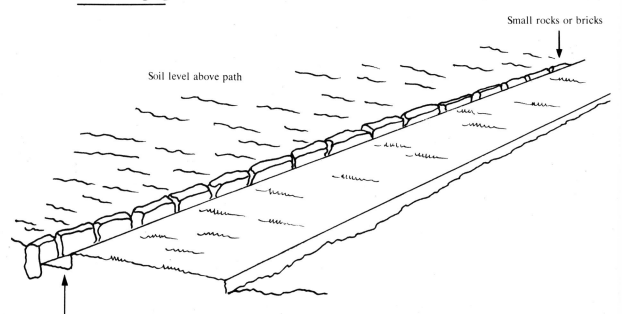

Small rocks or bricks

Soil level above path

Space between stone edging and grass path to avoid damage to lawn mower. Not necessary for other types of path

A garden in a trough

Two other means of growing alpines may appeal especially to those who have virtually no garden space—or where gardening as such is not possible. One or more troughs take up very little space on a patio, for example, but they could be a congenial home for a wide variety of choice, slow growing plants. As antiques, real stone troughs are expensive nowadays, but cost much less in modern substitute material in which plants will grow just as well. Troughs should be no less than 6 in. deep inside—better 8-10 in. or more—and must have a drainage point. If there is only one hole at the end, the trough should be slightly tilted towards it, whether or not the trough is raised above the ground level. A 1/2-1 in. covering with stone chippings after planting is advised. Assuming one wishes to plant slow growing subjects, the soil should be of a gritty mixture as for scree with a few broken bricks as a bottom layer. As for larger beds, stones are optional, and can be dispensed with for the sake of space. A stone or two would be needed, however, if part of the surface is to be raised, otherwise it can be more or less level, with the plants themselves preventing a flat appearance. A dwarf conifer would achieve this, but it would have to be a very slow grower, such as *Juniperus communis* 'Compressa'. Space between plants should be about 4-5 in. for the very close growing, and if some of a more prostrate or trailing nature were planted to hang over the rim of the trough, the effect would be enhanced.

An alpine house interior showing that contents can include shrubs also. In this example, both pans and rock are used with good results. The drooping-leaved Acer palmatum 'Dissectum' provides some shade and gives a cool effect. In pans, Sempervivum a. laggeri is in front of red rhodohypoxis and pink Erodium chamaedrioides, which are not reliably hardy outdoors.

Alpine house

An alpine house, is yet another means of growing a collection of choice subjects, especially those allergic to wet winters. It can be of any size, unheated, but with ample ventilation which should be open except during very severe or stormy spells. The bench should be at a convenient height and made of a durable material to take fine pea gravel on which to stand the plants in pots or pans. Some alpine enthusiasts construct a miniature rock garden on the bench, using feather rock for lightness and for actual growing, since the roots of plants can penetrate its porous structure. Although this is a special way to grow alpines, often attracting the connoisseur, there is no reason why anyone else to whom alpines appeal should not invest in an alpine house. A great deal of pleasure could be gained thereby, and virtual freedom from the vagaries of adverse weather is an added incentive. The roof would, however, need to have some shading against the sun in summer, and the best form of shading is the kind one can roll up or down with a cord on the principle of a venetian blind. It is made of split cane or of thin plastic strips.

How to choose and plant alpines

Having already emphasized the importance of selecting a site, carefully taking account of suitability, some advice will be helpful on making a selection of plants. In doing so, some readers may find plant names a formidable obstacle, but it need not be. The first thing to accept is that all plants have names by which they are internationally known. To depart from this and to attempt to apply a folk or common name would result in confusion. A folk name often applies to only one of many species in a genus. The genus, or generic name always comes first. Take for example *Campanula* which covers the folk name of harebell and bellflower. The specific name comes next, and if one has the true harebell it is *Campanula rotundifolia,* but there are hundreds of other species which have no folk name. A cultivar is a form, variety or clone of garden origin, and takes third place, hence a white form of harebell in cultivation is *Campanula rotundifolia* 'Spetchley White'. Both Latin and Greek are used in plant names, and the specific name often describes some distinguishing feature. Campanula refers to the bell-type flower (as in *Campanula* and campanology), while *rotundifolia* can be seen as having rounded (rotund) leaves. Plant names become interesting once their necessity is accepted. Identification is also easier if the correct name is known.

The most important factor in making a selection is to choose kinds best suited for a given site. Success depends upon this suitability to soil, climate, or whatever, as described in the general list of recommendations. Many are widely adaptable, but some are over-endowed with vigor which could endanger slow growing kinds if planted too close to them. A few are so invasive that they should be avoided altogether and these are mentioned. In this connection, it can be risky to accept gifts or otherwise acquire plants without knowing what their growing habits are. This emphasizes the importance of making a selection with care, as

Many bulbous and shrubby subjects contribute to the variety in an alpine house. Bulbs and corms often have a long period of dormancy which can result in gaps in an outdoor planting scheme, whereas, indoors, this problem does not arise.

Stone trough or sink converted into a miniature rock garden

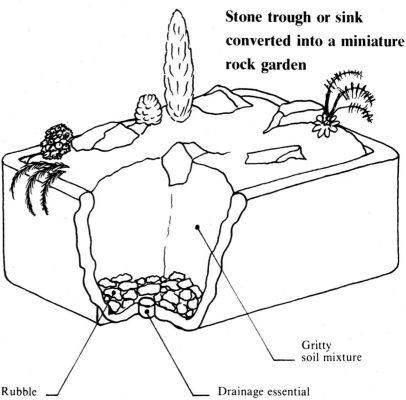

Gritty soil mixture

Rubble

Drainage essential

16

well as of segregating when planting those with vigorous spread, from the choicer, slow growing kinds.

Without any doubt the best selection of plants can be made from a specialty catalog, or from noting the names of those seen in other gardens. In most gardens, both public and private, established plants can be seen and fully appreciated, which is more than can be said in the case of hastily planted exhibits at flower shows. In garden centers, there is seldom a wide variety offered, but at least one is able to see them in flower, and take away for immediate planting.

There is no hard and fast rule as to planting time for alpines. If the plants one selects are pot grown, then it can take place virtually at any time except when very wet or frosty weather prevails. Generally speaking, early autumn or spring are the best times for planting, but much depends on the site being well prepared. For smaller, bare-rooted cuttings and seedlings, site preparation is more critical unless conditions are perfect. Slow growing plants, not grown in pots, may not survive in either a dry summer if planted in spring or a harsh winter if planted in autumn. Planting is a very simple matter. The routine is to make holes with a trowel, remove the pot and insert. Always see that plants are well watered beforehand, and if planting into very dry soil, fill up each hole with water with the plant in position before drawing back the soil and firming in.

Most people embarking on alpines will prefer to have one of a kind for the sake of variety. Indeed this would meet any need where small beds or rock gardens are concerned. For larger areas, groups of not less than three of a kind will give a more spectacular display. For interest's sake, labeling each kind should not be scorned. Names at first might appear unimportant, but the greatest pleasure in gardening with alpines comes to those who know their plants. To know them is to love them, and to love plants is a very precious gift—an antidote to the pressures of modern life.

It will not often occur, or be necessary for amateurs to propagate alpines. Some will naturally wish to raise some from seed as a cheaper method than buying flowering-sized plants. Some will breed true from seed, others will come as a mixture of colors—including the popular aubrieta, some dianthus and helianthemums. Others will come true, but seed may be difficult to obtain, or may take a long time to germinate and need special care. In a general way, an attempt to furnish a rock garden from seeds is not likely to be successful in terms of satisfaction compared with an outlay on plants. This may well prove more economical in the long run. It is, however, good fun to raise seeds occasionally, and to take cuttings. The descriptive list gives the best method of increase for most kinds.

A little more care in placing plants here would have given more pleasing results. The two white-flowered plants (top) should have been separated more widely with, perhaps, something blue between them.
Below, the scarlet Penstemon pinifolius should not have been next to the salmon-red dianthus. Both tend to hide the low growing, grey Sedum s. 'Capablanca' behind. The bronzy-purple-leaved acaena will soon overrun both this and the slow growing saxifragia (center, right).

This could be a 'walkabout bed' of mainly close-growing alpines. There are sedums and sempervivums with the large green and mahogany rosettes of Sempervivum 'Commander Hay' in flower during June. The close, deep green carpet of Arenaria balearica (top right) will cover low rocks as well as soil and contrasts well with silvery-leaved plants.

An A - Z list

Explanation of symbols

○   Mainly sunny position essential

◐   Part shade preferred

◑ ●   Part or full shade preferred

●   Full shade essential

No symbol indicates adaptability to full sun or part shade

A pleasing foliage effect is shown with the silvery artemisia behind a dwarf violet-purple Salvia 'May Night' and the green of a hebe. In front is a fine clump of Pterocephalus parnassii.

Concrete is better than nothing for walls and raised beds. With a wider variety of plants the block wall could have been hidden almost entirely by flowers and leafy climbers.

Acaena
(Rosaceae)

Acaena microphylla

Achillea ○
(Compositae)

These give good foliage cover and a show of yellow or white flowers on flattish heads in summer. *A. argentea* has tufty silver foliage 4 in. high, with heads of white flowers at 6 in. *A. aurea* and *chrysocoma* are much alike with a vigorous spread of soft light greenery, topped with bright yellow heads to 8 in. *A. tomentosa* is closer growing with darker greenery and deeper yellow flowers June to August at 8 in. *A.* 'King Edward' has very pleasing primrose-yellow flowers for most of the summer. All the above need very good drainage, but are easy to increase by division in spring or early autumn. Achilleas are effective with campanulas.

Achillea tomentosa

Vigorous carpeting plants giving good foliage cover, which will grow in almost any soil. *A. buchananii* makes a dense mat of soft, pea-green foliage. *A. inermis* of similar habit is bluish-bronze and *pulchella* reddish-purple. All these are better as paving plants, for flowers are insignificant. *A. microphylla* is outstanding for its russet-brown mats and bright red burr-like flowers blooming into late summer. *A. adscendens* grows taller to 6 in. with arching stems carrying grey-green leaves and reddish burrs—good as groundcover; while 'Blue Haze' will inhabit a wall. Acaenas can also be used as summer cover for spring flowering bulbs. All are easy to increase by division in spring.

Adonis
(Ranunculaceae)

These are choice slow growing plants, with the one fault of some being a long dormant period. They need good but well drained soil, but take well to peat beds. *A. a.* 'Fukujukai' from Japan has the distinction of being the first dwarf perennial to flower. In February-March come rounded greeny-yellow flowers, opening at 2 in. to glistening sulfur yellow and followed by ferny foliage. Height 4-6 in. becoming dormant in May and June.

A. amurensis 'Plena' flowers February to April, with fine double, greenish-yellow flowers 6 in. tall. Both are increased by division in early autumn when the clumpy plant is large enough, but *A. vernalis* is slower to increase. Its charming yellow flowers come on ferny-leaved bushy growth, March to May; 12-14 in. tall where happy. *A. volgensis* is similar, but a week or two earlier to flower. So long as the adonis are not smothered, ajugas are attractive in association.

Adonis amurensis 'Plena'

Aethionema 'Warley Rose'

Aethionema ○
(Cruciferae)

These sun-lovers are best in poor or stony soil, and are excellent wall plants. *A. grandiflorum* and *A. pulchellum* are much alike with a low twiggy habit, bluish foliage to 10 in. smothered in rounded spikes of clear, light pink flowers in early summer. They may be raised from seed, but the cultivars 'Warley Rose' and the slightly deeper pink 'Warley Ruber' can only be increased from summer cuttings under glass. Both have intense pink flowers above the blue-grey foliage on compact 6 in. bushy growth.

Ajuga ◑
(Labiatae)

They make attractive leafy mats of real value when not too dry. All have short flower spikes in spring and early summer. All form rosettes of shiny leaves rooting as they spread, making for rapid increase. Useful under deciduous shrubs and pleasant in association with silver or gold foliage. *A. reptans* has several cultivars, including white and pink-flowered, as distinct from the basic blue type. 'Burgundy Glow' has crinkled, shiny foliage variegated pink, bronze and cream with *A. reptans* 'Multicolor' ('Rainbow') having several shades; both have blue spikes in spring. 'Pink Elf' is a dwarf form, and *A. reptans* 'Variegata' spreads quickly by runners, with creamy-marked leaves. *A. metallica* has dense, shiny crinkled leaves of deepest blue and *A. pyramidalis* is best for flowering with spikes of gentian blue to 8 in., but needs a damp soil.

Ajuga reptans 'Burgundy Glow'

Allium oreophilum ostrowskianum

Allium
(Liliaceae)

Only the smallest, non-invasive species can be recommended, as members of the bulbous onion family. All have heads sometimes dangling with small, brightly-colored flowers. Some have a long period of dormancy but all are readily increased by division when dormant. *A. cyaneum* and *A. beesianum* are both excellent for their sheaves of blue flowers on 4 in. stems. *Allium oreophilium ostrowskianum* has tufts of narrow leaves with umbels of broad carmine-red flowers. *A. moly,* a yellow species, should be avoided, being invasive, but *A. cyathophorum* 'Farreri' is recommended for its heads of purple flowers, 6 in. *A. narcissiflorum* is only 4 in. with nodding bells of wine red, while *A. pulchellum* has quite large heads 6 in. tall of deep pink. All these alliums are summer flowering, and are best combined with plants of a mounded or cushion habit, such as the dwarf dianthus.

Alyssum ○
(Cruciferae)

A. saxatile and its variations are showy and deservedly popular for spring display. They form robust mounded to spreading growth above ground from a single nonspreading root system with sprays of small flowers in yellow shades, covering the greyish foliage. The yellow species are easily raised from seed, but variations come from cold frame cuttings in late summer or autumn. *A. saxatile* is offered in *A.s.* 'Compactum', but is not really compact when old as is the cultivar 'Gold Ball'. Both are bright yellow, but *A. s.* 'Citrinum' is a lemon yellow, and 'Dudley Neville' a primrose yellow. The double-flowered *A. s.* 'Plenum' is very showy with fuller flowers, but is less vigorous. All the above need sun, like lime and good drainage.

Alyssum saxatile 'Citrinum'

Alyssum saxatile

23

Anacyclus ○
(Compositae)

A. depressus is not long lived and needs sharp drainage or scree soil. It forms flat rosettes of finely cut leaves producing large white, daisy flowers which are crimson underneath. Only about 3 in. high, flowering in early summer, it can only be increased by seed. Looks fine with *Myosotis rupicola*.

Androsace ○
(Primulaceae)

These plants are widely distributed in nature. Most of them form hummocks of rosettes, some grey green and are easy in very well drained soil. Rounded heads of mostly pink flowers come in early summer. *A. sarmentosa (primuloides)* is the best known of this

Anacyclus depressus

type, growing 2-4 in. tall, with the cultivar 'Watkinsii' having rosy-red flowers. *A. sempervivoides* is also attractive. *A. villosa* and *A. microphylla* are smaller, both safest in scree conditions, but *A. lanuginosa* and its cultivars are distinct. They have silvery trailing stems carrying heads of pink or near-white flowers in later summer. These are good subjects for a sunny wall. They are best increased from cuttings, but the rosette-forming kinds will divide, providing pieces detached have sufficient root to survive.

Andryala ○
(Compositae)

A. aghardii needs a warm place and very good drainage to show off its silvery tufts of foliage set with vivid yellow flowers for several weeks of summer. It grows 6-8 in. tall and can be increased from late summer cuttings or seed.

Androsace sarmentosa

Androsace lanuginosa

24

Anemone
(Ranunculaceae)

These differ widely in origin and cultural need. For sun or partial shade. *A. baicalensis* has large white flowers on 8 in. stems, and *A. magellanica* of similar height has cream flowers. A. *palmata*, 5 in., is a choice, yellow-flowered species needing full sun, and though the near-red *A. x lesseri* is tall at 12 in. it is a splendid plant. All the above flower in early summer, and can be increased by division when large enough. *A. nemorosa* is the wood anemone, easy to grow and naturalize. In a bed their roots, like tiny brown sticks, are difficult to find and plants should be sited where they can remain. The species with flowers of white or pale blue are best confined to a shady corner or to grow like snowdrops in grass. *A. n. robinsoniana* is a fine blue and *A. n.* 'Alba Plena' is an outstanding double white. All grow 4-5 in. preferring heavy to very light soil. *A. ranunculoides* is of similar growth, but flowers are bright yellow. All have a long dormant period, and can be overplanted with the smaller ajugas.

Anemone ranunculoides

Anemone x lesseri

Anemone nemorosa 'Alba Plena'

Antennaria ○
(Compositae)

These are easily grown groundcovers, rooting as they spread with short, tufty, greyish leaves. Flowers are on little clusters in early summer. Useful for paving or as cover for alpine bulbs, which will grow through the carpet of the smaller growing types.

A. aprica is vigorous with greyish foliage and white flowers to 6 in. *A. dioica* is seen in white, pale pink and rosy-red variants, all 4 in., but *A. d.* 'Minima' is a distinctive pink dwarf. All are easily divided in spring or early autumn, and look well close beneath dwarf shrubs and conifers.

Anthemis (Compositae) ○

These are easy in any well drained soil, but white-flowered *A. cupaniana,* though showy and long flowering, spreads too quickly for small beds. It has finely divided leaves, as has the less rampant *A. triumfettii. A. pedunculata* 'Tuberculata' also white flowered to 8 in. is grey-leaved with clumpy growth. The most valuable as an alpine plant is the silvery-leaved *A. rudolphiana (A. biebersteiniana)* with deep golden flowers. These are borne erectly to 6 in. and make a fine show in early summer. All the above can be divided or raised from seed. *A. nobilis* is the herb chamomile with aromatic deep green foliage. It grows close to the surface with a fairly rapid spread, and though the double white-flowered *A. n.* 'Plena' is of limited value as a garden plant, only 4 in. tall, the non-flowering *A. n.* 'Treneague' is used for lawns or as a walk-upon groundcover.

Antennaria

Anthemis cupaniana

Anthyllis ○
(Leguminosae)

Long lived, sub-shrubby plant of value in well drained sunny places, including walls. *A. hermanniae* makes a dense twiggy mound of greyish hue, with an abundance of small yellow pea-shaped flowers in summer. Height 8 in. *A. montana* is best in the deep pink to red *A. m.* 'Rubra'. It makes a surface spread of silvery leaves covered in early summer with clover-like heads to make a bright display 3 in. high. Seed increase is possible as is careful division in spring.

Anthyllis montana

Aquilegia glandulosa

Aquilegia ◑
(Ranunculaceae)

The columbines have a wide range in nature. Some of the dwarfest are best in scree soil, others prefer some damp and shade, but unfortunately few are long lived. They can only be increased from seed, and this does not invariably produce plants true to name, except in the dwarfest kinds. These include *A. bertolonii* with large blue flowers on 5 in. stems, and *A. discolor* blue and white, only 3 in. *A. scopulorum* has soft blue flowers and silvery foliage, 5 in. These three are best in scree or rock crevices. *A. flabellata* 'Nana', available in both blue and white, is most robust at 8 in. as is the charming blue and white *glandulosa*. These both like a cool position with peaty soil. All flower in early summer, and seed should be sown outdoors when ripe.

27

Arabis albida

Arabis ○
(Cruciferae)

Spring flowering plants with much the same general habit as *Aubrieta*, but *A. albida* and its double form, both white, are too rampant for small sites, although useful for banks or edgings. A cultivar named 'Rosabella' is more compact with pink flowers to 4 in., but *A. a.* 'Coccinea' and 'Rubra' are brighter and deeper colored. Well drained soil is essential for these and the rather short lived species. These make low hummocks, are dividable, and will come from cuttings in autumn. *A. ferdinandi-coburgii* 'Variegata' is tiny with white flowers above a mat of variegated foliage, rooting as it spreads. It grows 3 in. tall and is useful between rocks, through which early flowering bulbs such as chionodoxa will grow.

Arabis albida 'Rosabella'

Arenaria montana

Arenaria ○
(Caryophyllaceae)

Easy, close growing plants for early summer, nearly all white flowered. *A. balearica* is the only exception to a general preference for sun. It grows as a mere film of bright green, dotted with white flowers only 2 in. above. It needs a dampish, half-shady place, is quick to spread, but is not hardy in cold areas. *A. caespitosa* 'Aurea' is somewhat similar, but needs sun; it has permanently golden foliage and sparce white flowers. It needs to be frequently divided and replanted to retain color and compactness. *A. ledebouriana* has close grassy foliage and small white flowers, but the brightest is *A. montana* whose somewhat trailing deep green foliage is smothered in larger, pure white flowers in summer. Both are about 4 in.

A. pinifolia is also attractive, with a mounded, narrow-leaved growth.

A. nevadensis and *A. tetraquetra* make curiously attractive cushions, but are best in scree conditions. Both rank as collectors' items.

Arenaria caespitosa 'Aurea'

Arisarum ◐ ●
(Araceae)

A. proboscideum makes a low mass of arrow-shaped leaves in a cool, shady spot, through which appear what look like mouse tails, in early summer. A curiosity which dies back to dormancy from September to March.

Armeria maritima 'Dusseldorf Pride'

Armeria caespitosa

Armeria ○
(Plumbaginaceae)

Often called thrift, these are first rate alpines, giving excellent evergreen groundcover, like tufted grass, and a show of flowers in early summer on rounded heads. The choicest and slowest to grow, as low mounds is *A. caespitosa* with clear pink flowers only 2 in. tall. It needs well drained soil. *A. maritima* is a variable, easily grown species. The brightest and nearest to red is 'Dusseldorf Pride', 6-8 in. tall. 'Vindictive' is pink and 'Alba' pure white, 5-6 in. flowering in early summer. *A. corsica* is distinctive for its heads of brick-red color on 10 in. stems. All are easy to divide in spring or autumn, except *A. caespitosa* which is best from seed or base cuttings.

Arnebia ○
(Boraginaceae)

A. echioides, the intriguing prophet's flower, forms fleshy-rooted plants with hairy green leaves. It sends up clusters of bright yellow flowers in late spring, on which are maroon spots. Though not difficult in well drained light soil, this remains a rare and choice plant. About 10 in. high, it can be divided in autumn. It contrasts well with pulsatillas and *Phlox canadensis.*

Arnebia echioides

A closer view of the photograph on page 107 showing how Saxifraga fortunei 'Wada's Variety' is in danger of being smothered in the center with a quick growing ajuga.
The dangling yellow sprays on the left are of the charming Cotyledon simplicifolia.

Artemisia schmidtiana 'Nana'

Artemisia ○
(Compositae)

The only species recommended as an alpine is *A. schmidtiana* 'Nana' for a very well drained position. It forms a low mound of bright silvery filigree foliage, making a good background for other plants with colorful flowers. Its own flowers are greyish and of no importance. Increased by division in spring, or from summer cuttings.

Asarina
(Scrophulariaceae)

A. procumbens (formerly *Antirrhinum asarina*). This resents being sun-baked, but in a cool place spreads between rocks or walls to give a long succession of creamy-colored, snap-dragon-like flowers, 4 in. tall. Division in spring.

Asperula suberosa

Asperula ○
(Rubiaceae)

Includes some choice diminutive species, but *A. capitata* is easy to grow, forming slow-spreading 2 in. hummocks with tiny, shell-pink flowers in early summer. *A. lilaciflora caespitosa* makes a prostrate, deep green mat, set with clear pink flowers for many weeks, only 1¹/₂ in. *A. nitida* makes a dense green cushion studded with pink flowers, 3 in. tall. *A. suberosa* is a treasure, having more upright, grey-leaved stems to 2¹/₂-in., producing clusters of pink, tubular flowers in late spring. Both are best in scree-type soil and resent winter wet. Careful division in early spring.

Asplenium
(Polypodiaceae)

Two species of ferns suitable for shady
nooks and crevices. One is the dainty,
grey-leaved *rutamuraria* with deeply
cut rosette leaves. The other is *A.
trichomanes,* which is also evergreen
and rosette forming with fingered
bright green fronds.

Asplenium

Aster alpinus

Aster ○
(Compositae)

The few dwarf species of this genus,
which includes michaelmas daisy, are
worth considering. *A. alpinus* makes a
neat, easily divided clump, having
wide, yellow-centered daisy flowers in
spring and early summer. It is variable, with white, pink-lilac and blue
shades available to name. Height 6-8
in.
A. natalensis creeps to form mats of
deep green rosettes, with bright blue
flowers on 8 in. stems for many weeks.
A. sativus atrocaeruleus has smaller
sky-blue flowers for much of the summer from compact plants 6 in. tall. A.
spectabilis is autumn flowering from
mats of leathery leaves and sprays, 8
in. high of intense blue. All these are
fairly adaptable and easy from division. They are best in company with
yellow-flowered subjects.

Astilbe ◑
(Saxifragaceae)

Without exception, these like moist, humus-rich soil and some shade in return for a bright show of flowers between June and September. All have very attractive summer foliage even when not in flower, and though old plants divide readily, any obsolete woody root should be discarded when replanting. *A. crispa* has dark green, crinkly foliage in dense mound formation, above which come 5 in. poker-like spikes of bright pink in the best cultivar 'Perkeo'. *A. chinensis* 'Pumila' is very vigorous with lots of lilac-pink spikes in late summer, 8-10 in. *A. glaberrima* 'Saxosa' is the smallest, only 3 in. tall, a perfect miniature but demanding cooler conditions and preferring peaty soil. *A. simplicifolia* has a dwarf pink form 'Nana', only 5 in. tall, and has produced a splendid hybrid named 'Sprite'. This makes dark, finely cut foliage and gives a profusion of delicate, shell-pink flowers 8-10 in. high.

Astilbe crispa 'Perkeo'

Astilbe simplicifolia 'Sprite'

Aubrieta 'Dr. Mules'

Aubrieta ○
(Cruciferae)

Among the most popular of plants, these make a brilliant display in spring from March to June. They will come from seed, but not true to color. There is no excuse for retaining some of the older, paler shades with inferior flowers, when modern varieties are available either from seed or plants, by name and color. All they need is good drainage, but prefer soil to peat, and are partial to lime. As soon as flowering is over plants should be trimmed with shears. They will increase by division or cuttings in autumn. Named varieties offer ample choice of color.

A cascade of aubrieta

Bellis perennis 'Plena'

Bellis ○
(Compositae)

B. perennis. Two double daisies are included as dainty, reliable cultivars, much more in keeping than seed-raised strains. 'Dresden China' is clear pink, only 5 in. tall and 'Rob Roy' is deep red, 7 in. Both are free and long flowering, but are best divided and re-planted every year or two.

Blechnum ◑
(Polypodiaceae)

B. penna-marina is another diminutive creeping fern of bronzy green for crevices or shaded walls, with leathery fronds. *B. spicant* is larger with center fronds to 12 in., deeply divided, above a green rosette formation. Both are evergreen, but *B. spicant* will grow in sun where not dry. Division of all ferns is best in spring and summer.

Bolax ○
(Umbelliferae)

B. glebaria (Azorella trifurcata) is grown for its bright green rosette cushions, which steadily expand. These bear tiny yellow flowers. An easy plant for any well drained soil, which will respond to division in early autumn or spring.

Bolax glebaria

Blechnum spicant

Brachycome ○
(Compositae)

B. rigidula makes a 5 in. dark green mound, carrying lavender-blue, daisy flowers for many weeks. Comes from seed or will divide.

36

Bulbinella ○
(Liliaceae)

B. hookeri is a distinctive, semi-bulb-ous New Zealand plant with bronzy-green, narrow leaves. In early summer come stems to 12 in. of bright yellow, poker-like spikes. Increase is by seed or division.

Calamintha ○ ◑
(Labiatae)

C. nepetoides is fairly tall at 12-14 in., but makes a fine display in late summer of soft lavender-blue flowers for many weeks, in sun or partial shade. It is a trouble free plant of many uses, topping a wall or in front of perennials with a good upright habit. Divide in spring.

Calamintha alpina

Caltha palustris 'Plena'

Caltha ○
(Ranunculaceae)

As kingcup or marsh marigold, *C. palustris* is often seen and admired in the wild, but the more compact *C. p.* 'Plena' is a very good garden plant. So long as soil does not dry out in summer, it will give no trouble. In April and May it provides a bright display of fully double, deep yellow flowers on semi-prostrate sprays above its rounded leaves. Height 6-8 in. It is also seen in a single white form; but the best white species is *C. leptosepala*, with pure white sprays of open flowers on erect 5 in. stems in spring. Both can easily be divided after flowering and combine admirably with cardamines.

Campanula ○ ◑
(Campanulaceae)

A large and varied genus of great value, for most of them flower after the spring flush of alpines is over. Some species are very choice or difficult, others are short lived and a few are weedy. The varieties below are all worthwhile recommending as having reliability and merit, and include good cultivars, such as 'Birch Hybrid'. This flowers on and off for much of the year, forming neat clumpy plants with upturned flowers of deep lavender blue on 6 in. stems.

C. carpatica is best seen in its named varieties. All flower in the June to August period with mainly upturned cup or saucer-shaped flowers above bushy summer growth. 'Blue Moonlight' is china blue, and 6 in. tall. 'Chewton Joy' has a profusion of smaller, light blue flowers only 4 in. tall, 'Hannah' of similar habit, is pure white and 'Isobel' deep blue, growing to 8 in. C.

'Constellation' and 'Stella' are both hybrids of compact mounded habit with outspreading sprays of lavender-blue flowers for many weeks. C. garganica is of similar habit, but more tightly mounded, but there are taller variations as well as the choicer, deep lavender-flowered 'W.H. Paine'. These are good wall plants.

Campanulas with a creeping habit, dying back in winter, include the dainty blue cochlearifolia, the white 'Hallii' and larger, deep blue in 'Oakington', all 2½-3 in. 'G.F. Wilson' also runs below ground, to carry large violet-blue flowers 3-4 in. with pulla dangling purple-blue bells to 2½ in. and pulloides like a larger edition of it at 5 in. These types wander somewhat and may need curbing. Not so with C. portenschlagiana (C. muralis) which has clumpy growth and lavender-blue flowers about 5 in. useful in walls in

sun or shade. C. carpatica turbinata and its cultivars grow more like dwarfer carpatica types in shades of blue and violet. 'Molly Pinsent', 'Stansfieldii' and 'Norman Grove' are hybrids with clumpy growth, not evergreen, making a mounded display in varying shades of lavender blue in July and August. They are 4-8 in. tall. All the above are virtually trouble free in any well drained soil, lime or acid. The true harebell C. rotundifolia does not take well to cultivation though there are easier variations in deep blue and white in 'Covadonga' and 'Spetchley White'. One species to avoid for being weedy is C. poscharskyana. Campanulas can be divided in spring, and C. carpatica germinates well from seed, in mixture. All associate happily with dwarf shrubs and sedums, yellow or pink.

Campanula carpatica 'Blue Moonlight'

Campanula cochlearifolia 'Hallii'

Campanula carpatica

Campanula portenschlagiana (C. muralis)

Cardamine pratensis 'Plena'

Cardamine ○ ◑
(Cruciferae)

These all like moisture, whether in sun or part shade. They also respond to being divided and replanted after flowering every two years, and will then give a bright display in spring. The single flowered *C. pratensis*, known as the cuckoo flower, is often seen wild, but its double form 'Plena' is very attractive with erect 8 in. stems carrying lilac-mauve flowers. A more vigorous species with fairly rapid surface spread is *C. latifolia*, but it makes a splendid show of pale violet flowers on 12 in. stems. Both are excellent with calthas.

Carduncellus ○
(Compositae)

C. rhaponticoides is quite outstanding, with its evergreen rosette, up to 8 in. across, of leathery leaves close to the soil. In early summer comes a large, rounded, stemless head, like a ball of lilac blue. The plant is easy in well drained soil and the fleshy roots can be used as cuttings for increase.

Carex ○ ◑
(Cyperaceae)

This is sedge, and as a genus has little to commend it for garden cultivation.

Carex morrowii 'Evergold'

As a species *C. morrowii* is a useful evergreen groundcover, but the cultivar 'Evergold' *(C. morrowii* 'Aurea Variegata' *)* is outstandingly valuable. The bladed leaves of bright golden yellow with a thin green line, arch over to cover 12 in. or more across as a shapely mound, effective throughout the year, and only 6 in. high. It has many uses, among dark green dwarf conifers, or between red or blue flowering plants as an edging or even as a pot plant. Best divided in spring it is not fussy as to soil or position except a dislike of dense shade.

Carlina ○
(Compositae)

C. acaulis is a near relative of *Carduncellus* but with multiple thistle heads, stemless on low prickly growth. The form *C. a. caulescens* has stems 4 in. tall, having ivory-colored flowers in summer. Division or root cuttings.

Carlina acaulis

Cerastium ○
(Caryophyllaceae)

This genus includes the well known but pernicious snow-in-summer. Although it makes a bright show of white flowers above grey foliage it is so invasive that many a rock wall or garden has been ruined by it. The roots are very penetrating, and almost impossible to curb or eradicate without dismantling. It should never be introduced where other choice plants are to be grown, but there is one species worth having in *C. columnae,* which is an intensely silvery-leaved groundcover, with white flowers, and a modest spread above ground.

Ceratostigma ○
(Plumbaginaceae)

C. plumbaginoides is useful for banks, but not for small sites for its underground progress may be troublesome. It produces a carpet of leathery leaves and 8 in. stems tipped with sky-blue flowers in late summer. Leaves color in autumn. Easy to divide.

Cheiranthus ○
(Cruciferae)

As perennial wallflowers these are showy and some are perfumed. All prefer poor and dry soil to rich or moist, and in these conditions will live longer. Some are separated into the genus *Erysimum,* but are included here as being practically inseparable. *C. cheiri* 'Harpur Crewe' is an old-fashioned double yellow, sweetly scented with flowers above erect bushy growth to 14 in. *C. mutabilis* 'Constant Cheer' is basically violet mauve, tinged amber, and is seldom out of flower during cool weather. It grows to 10 in. *C.* 'Jacob's Jacket' is dwarfer and more spreading at 8 in., with heads of multicolored flowers in spring and early summer. 'Moonlight' makes a low spread of greenery to 6 in. covered in lemon-yellow flowers. 'Orange Flame' is quite descriptive, as is 'Sunbright'. The last three are all low growing and longer lived than the first three, for which autumn cuttings can be taken to renew old plants. Cheiranthus are good wall plants as one would expect, and look attractive with cytisus and helianthemums.

Cheiranthus 'Moonlight'

Cheiranthus cheiri 'Harpur Crewe'

Ceratostigma plumbaginoides showing autumn color

Chrysanthemum ○
(Compositae)

A few species are sufficiently dwarf to be considered but they bear little resemblance to the usual autumn and winter flowering kinds. *C. Hosmariense* has finely cut silvery leaves and in a warm sunny place or scree will flower continuously during cool weather. Flowers are 1½ in. across, pure white, and about 6 in. high. Effective against dwarf conifers. *C. Nipponicum* makes a steady spread of clumpy growth, dying back in winter. Its value is in the show of single white, pink-tinged, daisy flowers in autumn, 6-8 in. high.

Chrysanthemum hosmariense

Chrysogonum virginianum

Chrysogonum ○ ◑
(Compositae)

A single species, *C. virginianum*, begins flowering in May and continues until autumn, with 5 in. sprays of yellow above leafy clumps. It is not fussy as to position in sun or shade, but needs light, acid soil which does not dry out. Division is easy.

A section showing the brightness of early summer but signs of harmful competition are appearing. The blue Veronica prostrata is encroaching on a dianthus, with the deep pink Thymus d. 'Coccineus' spreading also from below. The intense white of Silene alpestris is effective, but the pleasing blue-grey rosettes of Sedum rhodiola have already flowered.

Codonopsis ○ ◑
(Campanulaceae)

This too has bell-shaped flowers like some campanulas but these are very distinctive in having exquisite markings inside. The flowers tend to droop from lax, tenuous stems. They are unusually distinctive, and are best planted where they can hang down a bank or over a rock wall. *C. clematidea* has light blue bells on 8-10 in. stems and *C. ovata* is somewhat similar at 6-8 in., flowering June to August. The fleshy roots do not respond to division, but plants may be raised from seed sown under glass.

Cotula atrata

Cotyledon simplicifolia

Cotula ○
(Compositae)

Mat-forming plants with *C. potentillina* and *squalida* being most often offered. They are useful only for paving, because of their vigorous spread of bronze-green foliage at ground level. *C. atrata* is less invasive and above the close mat of leafage produces 2 in. heads of browny red and flesh pink in bicolor. It needs well drained soil, sun and fairly frequent replanting.

Cotyledon ○ ◑
(Crassulaceae)

C. simplicifolia, sometimes listed as *Chiastophyllum oppositifolium*. This is one of the best of all rock garden plants, but it dislikes a very dry position. Otherwise it will grow in sun or shade. From rosettes of green, thinly succulent leaves it sends up 6 in. sprays on which dangle small yellow flowers for many weeks. It responds to top dressing with peat or soil as an alternative to replanting more deeply every two to three years. Easy to divide, it contrasts attractively with campanula and blue veronicas.

Crepis ○
(Compositae)

From among a welter of weedy species are two good garden plants. The finest is *C. incana,* which, with its fluffy pink flowers on 10 in. stems from June to September, is a first class plant. It has fleshy roots, which will produce root cuttings but has no outward spread from the clump of dandelion-like foliage. *C. aurea* has upright greenery, with sprays of very deep orange flowers at 8 in. from June to August. Plants divide readily in spring.

Crepis incana

Cyclamen coum

Cyclamen ◑
(Primulaceae)

A place may sometimes be found where some of the hardy cyclamen will flourish and add interest. All they need is some shade and good drainage. Most of them have flowers only 2-4 in. high, and when in leaf these too are attractive. Corms should not be planted more than 1 in. deep, and can be left as a permanent bed. They can only be increased by seed sown as soon as ripe. *C. cilicium,* is pink with marbled leaves. *C. purpurascens (C. europaeum)* has crimson, scented flowers and *C. hederifolium (C. neapolitanum)* in both pink and white are all late summer and autumn flowering. *C. orbiculatum* has several variations for late winter and spring flowering, and the larger but less hardy *C. repandum* is bright crimson, also in spring. They look attractive when planted with or beneath such dwarf shrubs as daphne, rhododendrons, azaleas and potentillas.

Delphinium ○
(Ranunculaceae)

Although the two dwarf kinds below are short lived—two to three years, they make a bright display and can be easily reproduced from seed. *D. chinense or tatsienense* make erect bushy growth covered in 10 in. spikes of brightest blue from June to August. *D. nudicaule* is unique for its orange-red flowers on 10 in. spikes over the same period. Both will flower in late summer from seed raised in spring, and both are effective between dwarf conifers.

Delphinium nudicaule (background) and Campanula carpatica 'Wheatley Violet'

Delphinium chinense 'Tom Thumb'

Dianthus plumarius

Dianthus ○
(Caryophyllaceae)

These are among the indispensables as alpines. Most are easy to grow in light soil, but a few are best as scree plants. The latter, where the tight mounded growth makes for difficulty with cut-

Dianthus 'Fanal'

Dianthus deltoides 'Flashing Light' is well situated here on a low wall. It flowers for many weeks in early summer and is easy to grow.

tings, will come true from seed, but there are dwarf strains of a mixture which also come quite well from seed. Otherwise, late summer cuttings or autumn division usually succeed, and they all like a sunny position and good drainage. There is such a wide selection of named cultivars, especially of the silvery-leaved type growing from

2-8 in. in height and flowering from June to August, that there is ample choice, from catalogs or garden centers. Some make a good close surface mat while others grow more compactly. The species *deltoides* is distinct with its trailing habit, green to bronze-purple foliage and small but very bright flowers in pink, red and glowing crimson scarlet. Any of those with outspreading growth are adaptable for walls and slopes. Colors range from white through pink to deep red, some with double flowers.

For scree beds, slow growing, choice species include *D. alpinus* with green leaves and large, deep pink flowers 2 in. high. *D. myrtinervis* is a very compact growing *deltoides* type, pink flowers 1 3/4 in. tall. *D. muralae* and *simulans,* make tight mounds, set with small, clear pink flowers 2 in. tall while *D. pavonius (D. neglectus)* has grassy tufts with quite large, rosy-red flowers. These and others for scree are best increased by seed.

Dianthus generally fit in easily with other subjects, especially campanulas.

Diascia
(Scrophulariaceae)

The species *D. cordata* has been discarded for the hardier hybrid named 'Ruby Field'. In a sunny situation this will give a long succession of salmon-rose flowers above low greenery to about 6 in. from June onwards. It tends to exhaust itself rather quickly and should be top dressed or divided, then replanted in spring if losing vigor. Combines effectively with *Gentiana septemfida*.

Disporum ●
(Liliaceae)

D. oreganum (D. smithii) is a humus-loving, lime-hating plant which is unusual for having conspicuous orange berries following greenish flowers. It grows erectly to 8 in. and the orange cherry-sized berries are long lasting, nestling in the green foliage until autumn. Old plants will divide in autumn and culture is not difficult in neutral or acid soil.

Dodecatheon
(Primulaceae)

These aptly named shooting stars have deeply reflexed petals with prominent yellow centers. There are several species which do not vary greatly, all having long leathery leaves and flowers hanging loosely in a clustered head 8-10 in. high in spring. They need no special soil, but resent very dry shade. All die back to dormancy from August to March and can be increased both from seed and division. Colors vary a little from pink to magenta crimson. The species *D. meadia* and *D. pulchellum (D. pauciflorum)* are most often offered. Effective among ferns are *Anemone nemorosa* and *A. ranunculoides*.

Diascia cordata

Dodecatheon meadia

Doronicum
(Compositae)

Easy to grow plants producing large yellow, ray-petalled flowers in spring. Some are too tall as alpines, but *D. cordatum* and *caucasicum* are only 6 in. tall, as is the spring cultivar 'Gold-lackswerg'. There is a fully double cultivar in 'Spring Beauty' which will reach 12 in. All flower from March well into May, and divide readily after flowering. They look pleasant with any blue or white spring flowers.

Doronicum caucasicum

Draba imbricata

Draba ○
(Cruciferae)

These are all spring flowering plants, most of them cushion-forming in small green rosettes. All need sun and good drainage.

D. aizoides has deep green rosettes, and makes a bright show of yellow flowers 3 in. tall. Of similar habit *A. dedeana* and *salomonii* have white flowers.

D. bruniifolia and *D. repens* are the easiest to grow, the latter spreading quite quickly, rooting down with short runners. Both are yellow and 2 in. tall. These are all increased by division or seed. For scree or an alpine house. *D. rigida*, *D. imbricata* and *D. mollissima* form very neat hummocks of slow growth, set with yellow flowers only 1-1½ in. All flower March to May.

Dryas ○
(Rosaceae)

Mat-forming plants with leaves deep green above and silvery beneath, producing large flowers of 'strawberry' formation, followed by fluffy seed heads. The best known—common in the European Alps is *D. octopetala*, but this does not flower so freely as *D. x suendermanii* and *vestita*. None has flowers more than 5 in. high. Cuttings in early autumn or seed.

er and less attractive with deep green narrow leaves. *E. caudatus (E. dalmaticus)* is about the best at 6 in. All species are best increased by seed.

Edraianthus pumilio

Epilobium glabellum

Epilobium ○
(Onagraceae)

One or two dwarf kinds of willow herb are worth growing where not too dry. *E. glabellum* makes a loose mound of greenery and has a profusion of ivory-white flowers 8 in. tall for much of the summer. *E.* 'Broadwell Hybrid' comes from a cross between this and the short lived pink species *kai-koense*. It has purplish-bronze foliage and creamy-pink flowers at 6 in. for many weeks. These may be increased by seed, cuttings in early autumn or division in spring. They look attractive with campanulas and summer flowering gentians. The species *E. macropus* should be avoided for its invasiveness.

Dryas octopetala

Edraianthus ○
(Campanulaceae)

The species *E. pumilio* forms tight silvery cushions set with violet-blue 2 in. flowers in spring and is best in scree soil. This is the species most often offered, but there are others a little tall-

Epimedium ◑ ●
(Berberidaceae)

The dwarfest of these are of real value in a cool position. They have very pretty foliage, forming a dome over their slowly expanding roots. Leaves are fresh until winter frost, and in spring comes the display of starry flowers followed at once by new foliage. None is fussy as to soil, though best where not dry.
E. alpinum makes rosy-purple flowers on wiry 8 in. stems, while *rubrum* is reddish pink. *E. grandiflorum* 'Rose Queen' grows compactly with a profusion of pink flowers only 6 in. tall. The best white is *E. youngianum* 'Niveum', with a neat habit and specially good foliage. Division in autumn is best, the roots being quite congested and tough. Epimediums have value as edging plants to a path where shady, and associate effectively with any blues, such as omphalodes and mertensia.

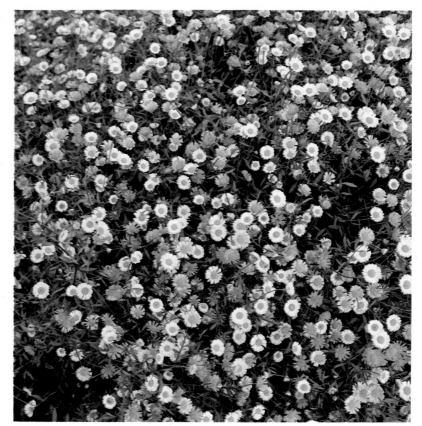

Erigeron mucronatus

Epimedium rubrum

Erigeron ○
(Compositae)

This varied genus includes some very dwarf species, but all have the typical rayed flowers. *E. aurantiacus* is unfortunately short lived, and its flowers are a bright, deep orange on 8-10 in. stems. Plants seldom flower for more than two seasons, but come readily from seed. *E. aureus* is also orange, only 3 in. tall from greyish tufts. It is best in lime-free scree, but the tiny, violet-flowered *E. leiomerus* is tolerant of any well drained soil. *E. simplex* makes a splendid show of pure white daisies from green clumpy growth at 8 in. *E. mucronatus* has a profusion of pale pink and white flowers on mounded twiggy growth for months—a good wall plant. Apart from the latter, these erigerons flower in early summer, but the hybrid 'Dimity' is at its best from June to August. This makes a sizable clump of soft green, and has arching sprays of pink, orange-flushed flowers. Though a little large for small sites, growing 8 in. tall and 10 in. across when in flower, it is a very showy plant. Most erigerons are best divided in spring or after flowering but *E. mucronatus* comes from seed, often self-sown.

Erinus alpinus

Erinus ○
(Scrophulariaceae)

The one species available is *E. alpinus* which varies in color but not in habit. They grow in compact, non-spreading tufted formation in any kind of soil and if not very long lived, are easily reproduced from seed. The type has lilac-mauve flowers on 2-3 in. spikes and *E. a.* 'Albus' is its albino. Most popular are the pink 'Mrs. Boyle' and the deeper rosy-pink 'Dr. Hanelle'. They are best in poor soil, and will grow happily in crevices and chinks.

Erodium ○
(Geraniaceae)

These also much prefer stony soil and full sun, and in these conditions are long lived. All have open saucer-shaped flowers and more or less ever-green foliage. *E. chamaedrioides* makes glossy green tufts, studded with white, pink-veined flowers for most of the summer, as does the pink-flowered *E. c.* 'Roseum'. Both are only 1½-2 in. high. *E. corsicus* is a little larger with greyish leaves and deep pink to red flowers, but is best in an alpine house. *E. guttatum*, *E. macradenum* and *E. supracanum* are much alike, all about 5 in. with ferny-grey foliage, light pink flowers, prettily veined purple. Growth is a little woody, but not so much as in the beautiful *E. chrysanthum,* which will mound up to 10 in. to carry lemon-yellow flowers. All these are very long flowering and deep rooting plants which can be divided with

care when old, or rooted from basal cuttings in a frame.
They associate agreeably with sedums and zauschnerias.

Erodium chamaedrioides

Erythronium ◑
(Liliaceae)

The common dog's tooth violet is *E. dens-canis* which has purple-rose flowers in spring on 6 in. stems. It has marbled leaves, but more desirable are some less known species. All are spring flowering bulbs with a long dormant period from July to early March. *E. californicum* also has handsome marbled leaves and large creamy flowers 6 in. tall with reflexed petals. *E. x* 'Pagoda' is yellow and *E. x* 'White Beauty' is also lovely. They need a cool but open soil, and if planted 4 in. apart will make a brave show as they increase naturally where suited. If interplanted in spring with dwarf mimulus, the blank spaces they leave in summer will be effectively filled.

Erythronium x 'Pagoda'

Euphorbia myrsinites

Euphorbia
(Euphorbiaceae)

This large genus includes very few species sufficiently dwarf and compact for small sites. These have a distinctive beauty. *E. cyparissias*, though growing only 6 in., is apt to spread too quickly below ground. It produces blue-grey, low needle-like foliage and heads of sulfur yellow flowers.
E. myrsinites can be well recommended for a sunny place in very well drained soil. It has prostrate stems from a central fleshy root which have succulent, bluish-grey leaves all the way up to a wide head of green tinged, golden-yellow flowers. It can only be perpetuated or increased by seed. Any self-sown plants which may appear should be moved into position when young. Old plants resent disturbance and will not divide. It associates well with dark-leaved dwarf conifers and hebes.

Euryops acraeus

Fuchsia 'Tom Thumb'

Euryops ○
(Compositae)

E. acraeus (E. evansii) is a low shrub-by plant with silvery foliage up to 12 in. tall, having bright yellow, daisy flowers in summer. It needs a dry situation and is attractive over winter. Seed or cuttings.

Frankenia ○
(Frankeniaceae)

Known as the sea-heath, *F. thymifolia* makes a close carpet of deep green only 1 in. high with a profusion of open pink flowers from June to September. It is best in dry or sandy soil and losses occur in cold wet areas in winter. Summer cuttings or division in spring.

Frankenia thymifolia

Fuchsia
(Onagraceae)

Although generally classed as shrubs or indoor plants those suitable for rock gardens,etc. can be grown outdoors in areas where freezing does not occur. If good pot grown plants are obtained in spring and inserted deeply, they can survive winter frosts, especially if on the south side of conifers, etc. In cold areas a covering of straw or leaves will help give additional protection. They flower from new growth and old stems should be cut back in spring. All flower from July onwards. *F. pumila* makes neat little bushes 6 in. tall with red and violet flowers. *F.* 'Tom Thumb' is a little taller and more robust with carmine-purple flowers at 8-10 in. Cuttings in summer.

A trough or sink can be used in even the smallest of gardens to provide continual interest.

Genista lydia

Genista ○
(Leguminosae)

All are shrubby, but some are quite prostrate and make a splendid display in early summer. *G. delphinensis* has large yellow flowers on tightly congested mats—best in scree soil, 4 in. *G. pilosa* spreads as twiggy evergreen mats with masses of yellow flowers, produced at 4 in. Best over a wall or bank. *G. sagittalis* does not flower so freely, making prostrate mats of flat stems to give evergreen and complete ground cover—like a larger *G. delphinensis*. *G. lydia* is larger, more like a cytisus (broom) and is a superb wall plant with pendulant sprays of light yellow flowers in early summer. Grows 12 in. tall.

Gentiana acaulis

Gentiana septemfida

Gentiana ○
(Gentianaceae)

This is a name almost synonymous with alpines, and no collection is complete without some of them. They are best divided into three groups, according to flowering time. Those that flower in spring like lime in the soil, though it is not essential. They also need a sunny position, as do the summer flowering species, which will grow well in either alkaline or acid soil. With one exception, however, the autumn gentians will not grow in alkaline soil and need a cool position away from strong sun in peaty or leafy soil. All need good drainage. *G. acaulis* is easy to grow, but is erratic to flower. No sure way of enticing it to flower profusely and regularly has been found. It makes clumpy growth at ground level of evergreen rosettes. The rich blue, trumpet flowers appear in spring, at 4 in. Clumps will divide but need to be planted very firmly. They combine happily with drabas, dianthus and erinus. *G. verna* is much smaller, with more open flowers of intense blue. It needs scree soil and appreciates the addition of cow manure. It is best increased by seed sown under glass after being frozen. The summer gentians are easy in any reasonable soil. The species *G. septemfida* is most often offered, flowering from June to August with loosely held blue trumpets to about 8 in. There are other species akin to this — mostly good garden plants, but not easy to divide, and best raised from seed.

Autumn gentians, the lime haters, grow with white thong-like roots, and have narrow grassy foliage stems terminating in 5 in. blue trumpets from August to October. Shades of blue vary from electric blue in the one lime-tolerant species *G. farreri*, to the deeper blue variations and hybrids of the best known *G. sino-ornata*. The roots will fall apart for multiplication, and it is good practice to replant in spring every two or three years. It is bad practice to plant where the soil can dry out or bake, and for a group they can be only 4 in. apart. These late gentians are ideal for peaty soils.

Gentiana sino-ornata

56

Geranium ○
(Geraniaceae)

The dwarfest of these true, hardy geraniums are invaluable for their adaptability, long life and long flowering. *G. dalmaticum*, in both shell pink and white, flowers in May from clumpy growth 4 in. tall. *G. cinerium*, with ash-grey foliage and pink flowers, is less often seen than the hybrids 'Apple Blossom', light pink and 'Ballerina' with large, open, lilac-pink flowers, prettily veined crimson. Both are 4 in. and deservedly popular, flowering from June to September. *G. farreri (G. napuligerum)* needs a scree soil to give its best; the stems are red and flowers soft pink with black centers. It flowers June to August. *G. sanguineum* is best in the form 'Lancastriense' being more compact with mounded growth up to 6 in. and covered in clear pink, open flowers. This is extra good when topping a retaining wall, as is the vivid magenta-purple *G. cinerium subcaulescens* at a similar height. The two go well together, especially if interplanted with blue campanula. A less vigorous *G. c. subcaulescens* is the warm pink *G. c. s.* 'Splendens'. Most of these hardy geraniums have woody roots, but old plants are capable of being divided. *G. sessiliflorum nigricans* makes a low cushion of small brown leaves, set with near-white flowers.

Geranium sessiliflorum nigricans

Geranium cinerium 'Ballerina'

Geranium subcaulescens

Geranium subcaulescens 'Splendens'

Geranium dalmaticum

Geum ○
(Rosaceae)

Only two of these are sufficiently dwarf to include. Both are easy to grow, flowering in early summer, and can be divided in early autumn. *G.x. borisii* has deep, bright orange flowers to 12 in. above soft green, leafy clumps. *G. rossii* is quite different with carrot-like leaves and yellow flowers. It also grows to 12 in. Both combine pleasantly with *Veronica teucrium* or *rupestris*.

Globularia ○
(Globulariaceae)

These are true alpines and of value for small sites, with low tufts of dark evergreen leaves. Flowers come as little blue fluffy balls in early summer. *G. incanescens* is a choice species best in scree conditions and flowers are bright powder blue only 2½-3 in. high. *G. cordifolia* and *G. meridionalis (G. bellidifolia)* are a little larger, of easy growth to 4 in., while *G. trichosantha* and *G. elongata* are both 6-8 in. Old plants are best divided in early autumn or spring.

Gypsophila ○
(Caryophyllaceae)

These are trailing plants, some too large for small sites, but still excellent for walls or where they can hang down. They are long flowering and long lived. *G. cerastioides* is distinct for not having a trailing habit but makes low mounds set with whitish-pink flowers. One of the finest trailing plants is *G. dubia,* which, with bluish-grey foliage and sheets of bright pink flowers, makes a splendid display. *G. repens (G. fratensis)* is very similar, as is *G.* 'Dorothy Teacher' though this is a little larger at about 4 in. *G. repens* and its forms 'Alba' and 'Monstrosa' are rampant. So is *G.* 'Rosy Veil', but its spread only lasts a season, as it dies back in autumn to a strong, deep rootstock. It is a good plant for a bank or wall top. All can be increased by cuttings or division.

Geum x borisii

Gypsophila repens 'Dorothy Teacher'

A very effective display for June to July, but soon the two main contenders for space will spoil one another. The pink dianthus (left) is already beginning to suffer, but the eventual victor in the competition is likely to be the silvery-leaved cerastium (top right) which spreads underground rapidly once fully established. Only C. columnae is safe to plant. The Sedum spurium (bottom) and the origanum (center) are surface spreaders and easy to curb.

59

Haberlea ●
(Gesneriaceae)

These are plants for cool shade, but
not to be grown under trees. A north-
facing aspect is best, preferably with
their leafy rosettes resting on or between stones. They also prefer leaf-
mold or peaty soil. Flowers are soft
lilac blue on short branching stems 4
in. high in May to June in *H. ferdinandi-coburgii*. *H. rhodopensis* has
somewhat smaller flowers of lavender
lilac and there is a white form of this
named *H. r.* 'Virginalis'. Haberleas
can be divided in late summer and
look fine with ferns, dicentra, dodecatheon, etc.

Haberlea rhodopensis

Hacquetia epipactis

Hacquetia ◑
(Umbelliferae)

The one species *H. epipactis* is best in
some shade and is included not only
because it grows well in dampish or
heavy soil and is long lived, but because it flowers in earliest spring. The
flowers are in sulfur yellow heads, 6
in. tall, and when these are over, there
comes a low canopy of green leaves
from its tough clumpy roots. Division
is best in autumn. It is adaptable for
use in peat beds.

Haplopappus ○
(Compositae)

H. lyallii makes 6 in. mounds of deeply
toothed, green leaves on which deep
yellow flowers come on short stems in
late summer, at a time when alpines
are less colorful. It needs very well
drained soil in full sun, and is effective
on top of a wall. Propagate from cuttings or division in spring.

Helianthemum ○
(Cistaceae)

The so-called rock roses are somewhat shrubby, but best included here as very popular and indispensable alpines. Most of those offered are cultivars in a wide variety of names and colors, from white to pinks, yellows, reds, orange brown and many intermediate and bicolor shades. There are also some double flowered kinds and many have silvery foliage. Some are of prostrate growth. Others are more mounded, up to 10 in. in height, but all respond to clipping back after their early summer flowering has ended. This promotes tidiness, some being of quite vigorous growth, and may result in a second flowering in late summer. None is difficult to grow and will flourish in quite dry or poor soil— their only dislike being wet conditions. All will come easily from cuttings under a frame, best taken after flowering or in early autumn. Only two distinctive species need be mentioned. *H. lunulatum* makes erect little greyish bushes about 8 in., covered for a long period in small, pure yellow flowers. *H. serpyllifolium* is also yellow, but its green growth is completely prostrate and it flowers in May and June. Helianthemums are so varied in form and color that they benefit from association with blue-flowered plants to give the complete color spectrum.

Helianthemum serpyllifolium

Helianthemum 'Chocolate Blotch'

Helianthemum 'Wisley Pink'

Helichrysum ○
(Compositae)

Some of these are also shrubby and have outstandingly silvered foliage which lasts the year round. A few are. however, too tender for cold areas, but all are best in sandy, well drained soil. *H. bellidioides* is mat-forming with white crispy flowers on 4 in. stems. It is of vigorous growth and fully hardy, as is the charming *H. milfordiae (H. marginatum)*. This makes a mat of silvery rosettes with stemless, crimson-flecked white flowers in late spring. Both are easy to divide for replanting. *H. virgineum* has larger rounded leaves, felted and silvery with buff-pink flower buds opening to creamy white on 8 in. stems in May and June. *H. frigidum* and a few others are best as alpine house plants, attractive the year round, but the tiny grey shrublet *H. selago* is more adaptable given sandy soil and full sun. It grows somewhat like a bushy tree cactus with tiny yellow flowers to 6 in. Taller, shrubby helichrysums are very showy and though less hardy, autumn cuttings under glass will insure against winter loss. One of the best is the silvery *H. alveolatum* which will grow to 24 in. with yellow flowers. Also yellow with grey foliage and curry scented is *H. angustifolium* 'Glaucum' growing to 16 in.

Helichrysum milfordiae

Hepatica ◑ ●
(Ranunculaceae)

In nature these are semi-woodland plants but are adaptable to more open situations having some shade. They have no dislike of lime in the soil, and are as happy in stiff loam as in a peaty mixture. In March *H. nobilis (H. triloba)* has small but bright, open flowers to 6 in. followed by a canopy of ivy-like leaves. The type is blue, but white and pink are sometimes seen. There also are some very rare and beautiful double forms of each. *H. transsilvanica (H. angulosa)* is a little later, with lighter blue flowers and tri-lobed leaves of a lighter green. 'Loddon Blue' is a good cultivar. Hepaticas expand very slowly and are also slow from seed. Division is seldom needed with such plants and though, when old can be divided, they may take a year or two to settle down again.

Hieraceum waldsteinii

Hieraceum ○
(Compositae)

Some species are weeds, but two are good garden plants for any sunny position. *H. villosum* has silvery, woolly leaves and a bright display of yellow dandelion-type flowers on 8 in. stems in summer. It is easy to divide or multiply from seed. *H. waldsteinii* forms rosette clumps of soft silvered leaves and has sprays of yellow flowers 10 in. tall. This, unlike *villosum*, retains its foliage over winter.

Hippocrepis ○
(Leguminosae)

Hepatica nobilis

The cultivar 'E.R. Janes' of *H. comosa* is an excellent groundcover for a sunny place and well drained alkaline soil. The green mats are covered in late spring with lemon yellow, pea-shaped flowers. Height is only 2 in.

Horminum ○
(Labiatae)

H. pyrenaicum is an evergreen rosette-forming plant with crinkled leaves making a mat of growth, though not invasive. It will grow in any garden soil, and is easily divided. The flowers, on 6-8 in. arching stems in June to July, are small and deep blue. There is a deep pink variation 'Roseum'. It is not a startling plant, but is trouble free.

Hosta ◑ ●
(Liliaceae)

The plantain lilies have become deservedly popular garden plants, but only a few are sufficiently dwarf to include as alpines. They prefer shade where the soil does not dry out and have both flowers and ornamental leaves. *H. minor* 'Alba' has pointed green leaves and pure white flowers in late summer 8 in. high. *H. undulata* 'Medio Variegata' has wavy-edged leaves with prominent yellowish streaks in the green and 14 in. flower spikes of mauve trumpets. *H. tardiflora* is among the smallest growing species and latest to flower. The lavender-mauve flowers come in September on 8 in. stems. Hostas respond to good moist soil with peat, which can be used as a mulch. Plants can be left alone for years, or they may be divided in early spring.

Hutchinsia ◑
(Cruciferae)

Demure evergreen, cushion-forming plants preferring a cool position. The leaves are dark shiny green, deeply divided, and the white flowers come as dainty sprays on 3 in. stems. *H. alpina* is most often seen, but *H. auerswaldii* is even more compact at 2 in. Both flower in May and June and can be divided in early autumn.

Hydrocotyle
(Umbelliferae)

H. moschata is a rapid spreading groundcover included only for its use as a paving plant. The flowers are of no consequence, but the leaves in tiny rosettes are bright green.

Hylomecon ◑
(Papaveraceae)

H. vernalis (H. japonicum) is a charming, unusual spring flowering plant for any cool soil or position. The flowers are as open golden poppies 1-2 in. across in April and May, amid pleasantly green foliage. Height is 5 in. The fleshy roots are apt to become congested with age, but are easily divided and replanted after flowering or in autumn.

Hosta undulata 'Medio Variegata'

Hylomecon vernalis

weeks from June onwards. Others less hardy and best in scree in frost-free areas or in an alpine house elsewhere, are the creeping *H. reptans* and *H. trichocaulon*. Both are deep yellow, while *H. cerastoides (H. rhodopaeum)* is quite hardy with clumpy upright, glaucous-leaved stems and light yellow flowers. Hypericums are best from summer cuttings under glass or from seed.

Hypsella ◑
(Campanulaceae)

H. reniformis (H. longiflora) is an easy to grow creeping plant, making close green growth at ground level and bearing little pinkish-white flowers for several weeks in summer. A good paving plant or in shady crevices.

Hypericum olympicum 'Grandiflorum'

Hypericum ○
(Guttiferae)

A genus which includes well known shrubs and a few good alpine plants, but some lack hardiness. The hardiest are those which are excellent for wall tops or in crevices. They include *H. olympicum*—often listed as *polyphyllum* (or *fragile*). The flowers are bright yellow with prominent stamens. In *H. o.* 'Grandiflorum' they are 1 in. across in golden yellow. All this type have glaucous foliage and woody growth. The lemon-yellow *H.* 'Citrinum' (or 'Sulfureum') should not be omitted. All flower from June to August, mounding up to 10 in. *H. coris*, of much neater habit, forms little erect bushes of dark green to 6 in. producing starry golden flowers for many

The intense white of Silene alpestris contrasts well with a variegated leaved red aubrieta with a dwarf white lavender behind. The hummock of hutchinsia between the lavender and the variegated euonymus is badly placed so far back and this too is white.

Iberis commutatum

Iberis ○
(Cruciferae)

The hardiest of these are all white flowered and outstandingly showy. The general habit is that of low, dense, shrubby evergreen growth, which is covered in spring with rounded heads of pure white. *I. sempervirens* and *I. commutatum* are evergreen and excellent for a wall top, capable of long life and hanging over with little or no attention needed. I. 'Snowflake' is more upright though still evergreen and mound forming to 10 in. with fine white heads from May to July. Both this and I. 'Little Gem' are more compact, but the latter is more bushy at 6 in. Division is possible but summer cuttings produce better plants. *I. saxatilis* is best in scree or as a trough plant. It is slow growing, quite prostrate and covers itself in white flowers only 1½ in. high. Increase only by cuttings.

Iris ○
(Iridaceae)

Several dwarf species are valuable for various situations and soils. *I. chamaeiris* is also listed as *I. pumila* and as a group they are like miniature bearded or June-flowering iris. They flower in April and May at heights ranging from 6-12 in. and are available in several named varieties. Colors range from white to pink, cream, yellow as well as blue and violet. While their period in flower is rather brief, they can provide color where their inclusion is not in conflict with purist views of alpine plants.

I. clarkei is a true species with neat erect foliage and 10 in. bright blue flowers, flecked and spotted, produced in June. *I. cristata* needs a cool moist soil to produce its dainty blue flowers at 6 in., but the form *I. c. lacustris* is only half the size. *I. graminea* tends to hide its reddish-purple flowers amid grassy foliage. These are scented, and grow to 6 in. *I. innominata* comes in variable color, apricot yellow in the type, but in among these appear lilac, purple and lavender. This species dislikes lime, as does the somewhat similar *I. tencea* with lavender-blue flowers, both reach 8 in. in height, flowering May and June. Seed raised plants are better than those from divisions. Otherwise all the above can be divided and replanted after flowering, and they associate effectively with primulas, campanulas and mimulus.

Iris danfordiae

Iris pumila

Jasione ○
(Campanulaceae)

Easy and distinctive plants in the somewhat similar species of *J. jankae* and *J. perennis*. They form evergreen rosette tufts which bear rounded, fluffy-blue heads from June to August on 6-8 in. stems. Any ordinary soil suits these. They can be divided or reared from seed.

Lamium ◑ ●
(Labiatae)

Most of these are much too invasive for rock gardens, though useful for ground covering in shade. There are, however, two non-rampant kinds which prefer both shade and good soil. *L. garganicum* forms leafy clumps set with clear pink fowers 8 in. tall for many weeks of summer. *L. maculatum* 'Aureum' is a plant used for its foliage rather than for its pink flowers, and has leaves of rich golden hue. It grows to 6 in. Although neither of these run about as does *L. maculatum* in its other forms, they steadily expand and may need curbing after two to three years.

Lamium maculatum

Lamium maculatum 'Aureum'

Lamium maculatum 'Beacon Silver'

Leontopodium ○
(Compositae)

The genus includes the true edelweiss *L. alpinum* with its grey leaves and curiously attractive white flowers. Although easy to grow, it is seldom long lived and seed is the means of reproduction. There are various geographical forms which are more reliably perennial, including *crassum* and *souleii*, not quite so conspicuous in flower. *L. aloysiodorum* is not outstanding in flower, but is lemon scented.

Leontopodium alpinum

Edelweiss in association with other alpines

Limonium ○
(Plumbaginaceae)

The miniature species of sea lavender are suitable subjects, but make no bright display with their tiny, deep blue flowers. Plants are of tufted, deep green leathery leaves and short sprays in late summer. *L. cosyrense*, which can only be increased by seed, is 4-6 in. tall. *L. bellidifolia* has violet flowers on 8 in. stems.

Linaria ○
(Scrophulariaceae)

These are not very long lived plants but will easily reproduce from seed. They have, however, a long flowering season and are easy to grow. *L. alpina* has blue-grey, fragile stems and leaves, with small flowers of bright colors. Most are violet and yellow. Bicolors are pink and yellow. Height is 2 in. *L. origanifolia* grows to 8 in. with deep violet and white flowers.

Linum ○
(Linaceae)

These sun-loving plants vary considerably with bright yellow, blue and white open flowers, but make little spread from the roots. They flower from May to August and are best in dry soil. They dislike winter wet. *L. perenne (L. alpina)* has quite large, salver-shaped blue flowers above narrow 8 in. foliage. *L. arboreum* forms a low, bluish-leaved, shrubby mound with flowers of pure yellow. Height is 8 in. *L. flavum* is similar but green leaved and less shrubby, 8-10 in. *L. suffruticosum salsoloides* is white and best in its dwarf form 'Nanum', growing almost prostrate. It is of similar habit to the charming light blue *L. extraaxillare*.

Linum arboreum

Liriope muscari

Liriope
(Liliaceae)

Here are long lived plants with grassy evergreen leaves, that are widely adaptable for sun or partial shade in any but wet heavy soils. *L. graminifolia* is mat forming, useful only for groundcover, as the flowers are insignificant. The bladed leaves are dark green and plants spread steadily. *L. hyacinthiflora (Reineckia carnea)* has more upright grassy foliage, half hiding the tiny spikes of fragrant flowers in April to May.

Height is 10 in. The most colorful flowers are seen in *L. muscari* which, though a trifle tall, grows compactly into a large mounded clump with arching deep green blades. The lilac-purple flowers come freely in close-set spikes 12-14 in. in late summer and autumn when color is scarce. These plants, though dividable, can be left alone for years. A dwarfed cultivar is *L.* 'Majestic' but this needs a hot dry place to induce its lilac-purple flowers to make a show.

Lithospermum ○
(Boraginaceae)

Lithospermum diffusum 'Heavenly Blue'

The cultivars 'Heavenly Blue' or 'Grace Ward' of *L. diffusum* make a brilliant display of blue where the soil is lime free. The deep green leaves on prostrate stems are slightly hairy, and the open blue flowers bloom from May to July or August. Plants will not divide, but will come from cuttings in summer under glass, which are sometimes needed when old plants become exhausted. They are attractive where they can spread over a wall and are happy in a mainly sunny position or in a peat bed. They associate well with dianthus and hypericums. *L. oleifolium* is more upright with greyish leaves and large, sky-blue flowers but needs a sheltered position or should be grown in an alpine house. Grows 6 in. tall, May to June.

Lysimachia nummularia 'Aurea'

Lysimachia ◑ ●
(Primulaceae)

L. nummularia 'Aurea' is the only worthwhile species, being the golden-leaved form of creeping jenny. It needs a cool shady place where its trailing stems, with occasional yellow flowers, can wander and root down. Any excessive spread is easily checked.

Lychnis viscaria 'Splendens Plena'

Lychnis ○
(Caryophyllaceae)

Although some species are truly alpine and brightly colored, a few are so short lived as to be little more than annuals. They are all easy to grow in any well drained soil. *L. flos-jovis* 'Hort's Variety' makes soft silvery tufts and 8 in. spikes of brightest pink flowers in early summer. *L. x arkwrightii* is outstanding for its brilliant vermillion flowers above deep purple foliage about 10 in. tall. It is a cultivar from *L. x haageana* of similar color, but with green leaves. *L. viscaria* has deep green tufts and sticky stems carrying pink (or white flowers n *L. v.* 'Alba') but the showiest is *L. v.* 'Splendens Plena'. This has large double pink flowers, like small carnations, on 10 in. stems in June to July. The latter will divide in early autumn or spring but the others are best from seed, as are the two short lived species having bright pink flowers. *L. alpina* and *L. lagascae (Petrocoptis glaucifolia)* both only 4 in. tall, flower from May to July. All like sandy or light soil and associate pleasantly with campanulas.

Lychnis x arkwrightii

A corner piece in June to July when the spring flush is over. It shows the value of campanulas at this period, with the white C. carpatica (above) contrasting well with the lavender-violet C.c. turbinata (below). The rosettes of Sempervivum 'Jubilee' have produced several red-stemmed heads of pink flowers, while Arenaria pinifolia, behind, has nearly finished and Thymus praecox has reverted to its grey-green carpet hanging over the wall. Some attention will be needed here soon to prevent the little Juniperus communis 'Compressa' from being spoiled by the exuberant growth of surrounding plants.

Mazus
(Scrophulariaceae)

The two species are both good carpeting plants for any but the driest situations. *M. pumilio* has stemless, lavender blue and white bicolor flowers above close green foliage only 1 in. tall, while *M. reptans (M. rugosus)* has mauve and white flowers with bronzy-green leaves. Both are so filmy that they can be used for paving and as cover plants for bulbs.

Mentha ◑
(Labiatae)

M. requienii is of even smaller filmy growth with tiny round leaves and almost microscopic lavender-blue flowers. Its other distinction is the strong mint aroma which a touch or tread will induce. It is not hardy but in some areas it usually survives to spread quickly again in summer in any cool position. Other menthas are too large or rampant.

Mertensia ◑
(Boraginaceae)

Only two species are sufficiently dwarf and both prefer a shady position, though they are not difficult to grow. Both are mat forming, with rounded or tongue-shaped leaves, which fade in autumn. In spring come sprays of intense blue flowers, mid blue in *M. primuloides* and violet blue in *M. coventryana*. Plants respond to mulching and the latter has a fairly rapid spread.

Micromeria ○
(Labiatae)

These are very dwarf and somewhat shrubby plants. All have aromatic foliage and are best grown in light soil and full sun. *M. corsica* makes tight silvery hummocks 2 in. high, set with tiny bright pink flowers for many weeks. *M. illyrica* has dark green foliage and blue flowers in late summer. Grows 6 in. tall. Plants can be divided in spring.

Mimulus
(Scrophulariaceae)

Notable for having lipped, trumpet-shaped flowers in some brilliant colors. All the mimulus here like moist, but not boggy soil, and mainly sunny situations. Most of them form shallow rooting mats which are best divided and replanted in enriched soil in late summer or spring. A few can be raised from seed sown under glass and they will also come from summer cuttings of basal growth. *M. cupreus* is the parent for most of the colorful named cultivars with a mat-forming growth. *M. burnetii* has brown-orange flowers on 8 in. stems, and pure bright yellow of similar height in *M. langsdorffii*. Bicolor flowers in maroon and yellow come in M. 'Shep'. A little dwarfer at 6 in. 'Wisley Red' is very showy and 'Whitecroft Scarlet' is nearer vermillion in color, only 4 in. tall. The last two are much less vigorous but as with others it is a good plan to cut back after the first June to July flowering and top dress with fertilized sandy peat to promote new basal growth which may result in a second flowering. The diminutive yellow species *M. primuloides* is pretty but not fully hardy. Mimulus associate successfully with the taller primulas and dwarf astilbes, but are not suitable for raised beds.

Mimulus burnetii
'A.T. Johnson'

Mitella ◑ ●
(Saxifragaceae)

These are grown more for their ever-green foliage cover than for their tiny, brownish-green sprays of flowers. The plants make leafy mounds 4 in. high and are among the few kinds at home in quite dry soil in shade, as well as in more open positions. *M. breweri* has glossy mounded foliage and 6 in. flower sprays, but *M. caulescens* has a quicker spread closer to the surface in light green. Both are easy to divide and the latter will give cover to bulbs.

Moltkia ○
(Boraginaceae)

M. intermedia was formerly known as *Lithospermum intermedium* and is a splendid subject for a sunny place and sandy soil, not objecting to lime. It mounds up to 8 in. and has short sprays of small, bright blue flowers from May to July. Increased by basal cuttings or careful division.

Moltkia intermedia

Mimulus 'Shep'

Mimulus burnetii

Morisia ○
(Cruciferae)

M. monanthos (M. hypogaea) is rewarding for its bright yellow flowers in spring almost at ground level from a compact tuft of green jagged leaves. It needs scree or well drained soil and is excellent in troughs with *Gentiana verna* for company. Propagation is by root cuttings in early spring.

Myosotis ○
(Boraginaceae)

M. rupicola is a little forget-me-not which is perennial, though seldom living beyond three years. The flowers are intensely blue, on 4 in. sprays from a leafy tuft, April to June. This, too, needs sandy soil and is useful for troughs. Comes true from seed.

Myosotis rupicola

Oenothera ○
(Onagraceae)

A genus which embraces both perennial and biennial species including the evening primrose. The best dwarf perennials have a long display of yellow flowers, except for *O. taraxacifolia* which has large shaggy white, pink-tinged flowers on prostrate stems with jagged leaves. This is best in poor dry soil and is renewed from seed as is *O. acaulis*, with stemless yellow flowers. Both flower from June to August. Also for a dry open soil but with too much summer spread for confined spaces is the splendid *O. missouriensis*. Its fingered roots do not spread, but a single plant can cover a wide area of purely summer growth, prostrate and leafy. The flowers from June to September are large, reddish in the bud but pure lemon yellow when open. An excellent plant for a dry sunny slope. *Oenothera caespitosa* has neat clumpy growth with large white flowers on short stems while *O. riparia* has a leafy-mounded spread of about 12 in. across and is 8 in. tall, producing pure yellow flowers, June to September. *O. glaber* has rich golden-yellow flowers 1½-2 in. across on 12 in. stems with bronzy-green foliage. It is attractive and reliable if not too tall. These tufty species are best divided in spring.

Oenothera caespitosa

Omphalodes ◐
(Boraginaceae)

Omphalodes cappadocica

Carpeting plants showing kinship with myosotis, but these below are fully perennial and good hardy groundcovers in any ordinary soil. *O. cappadocica* is evergreen, with ribbed grey-green leaves and has sprays of bright blue flowers in spring. *O. c.* 'Anthea Bloom' is very free flowering in sky blue. Both grow to 6 in. These flourish with minimal attention for several years with slow spread, but *O. verna*, seen in both blue and white, is more rampant and does not retain its leaves beyond summer. It flowers briefly in April, growing to 4 in. Both are best divided in early autumn, and all respond to an occasional light mulch.

Onosma ○
(Boraginaceae)

The best known of this small genus, liking well drained soil, is *O. tauricum*. It has hairy narrow leaves of grey green forming a mound from a tap root. The flowers are light yellow and tubular, dangling from 10 in. stems May to July. Seed is the only means of continuity when plants are exhausted. A pink-tinged species of similar growth is *O. albo-roseum.*.

Ophiopogon ◐
(Liliaceae)

These are closely related to liriope and have evergreen grassy foliage and short spikes of tiny purple flowers in summer. The most outstanding is *O. planiscapus nigrescens*, for the 4 in. foliage is almost black. It makes a slow spread from underground shoots and can be left alone for years except for an occasional mulching of peat. The green *O. planiscapus* is useful only for groundcover, and in the narrow green leaves of *O. japonicus* nestle tiny spikes of white flowers, growing 4 in. The variegated form is less hardy.

Ophiopogon planiscapus nigrescens

Onosma taurica

Origanum ○
(Labiatae)

These are distinctive for having nepeta-like flowers in late summer. The most attractive need a very well drained soil and resent winter wet. *O. hybridum* has woolly grey-green leaves from a compact root and wiry sprays carrying rosy-purple flowers July to September, 6-8 in. tall. *O. scabrum pulchrum* is quite sturdy, forming clumpy plants on which appears a profusion of pale pink, green-tinged bracts in late summer, 6 in. tall. The large hop-like flowers of *O. rotundifolia* are creamy green on 5 in. stems. All are long lived where suited and can be divided in spring.

Origanum scabrum pulchrum

Othonnopsis cheiriifolia

Othonnopsis
(Compositae)

O. cheiriifolia is a sub-shrubby plant for a warm position having mounded grey-blue, somewhat succulent foliage and yellow flowers for several weeks of summer. Grows 8 in. tall. Although evergreen it is too tender for cold areas.

Ourisia ◑
(Scrophulariaceae)

Mat-forming plants for moist or peaty soil which does not dry out. *O. coccinea* has bright green leaves from surface-rooting plants and scarlet flowers dangling from 8 in. stems at intervals during summer. It is not very free flowering and appreciates a top dressing of peat. Not hardy in very cold areas. *O. macrophylla* is also a little tender but is otherwise robust with dense, deep green, rounded leaves and a striking display of pure white flowers in early summer. Both are easy to divide.

Oxalis
(Oxalidaceae)

A genus which includes two or three species of troublesome weeds, as well as some good garden plants. *O. adenophylla* has tufts of crumply grey leaves and larger funnel-shaped flowers of lilac pink, 2 in. in late spring. This and the white *O. enneaphylla* are best in scree or sandy soil. *O. inops* is pretty but is invasive and should be avoided. *O. magellanica* makes a neat carpet of bronzy lobed leaves and small round white flowers, produced on 1 in. stems for much of the summer. It is best in a less sunny, moist position. *O. articulata (floribunda)* is happy in dry soil and is very adaptable. It makes a mound of shamrock-like year round greenery, and stems 6 in. tall carry loose heads of bright pink flowers from May to August. The roots are like congested corms but are easily divided.

Oxalis adenophylla

Papaver alpinum

Papaver ○
(Papaveraceae)

Two diminutive species of poppy are worthy of note, in spite of being short lived. *P. alpinum* grows like a miniature Iceland poppy *(P. nudicaule)* with single flowers rising from a blue-green tuft to 5 in. from May to August. This comes only from seed as a miniature in white, yellow and orange shades. *P. miyabeanum* makes a mound of lobed greyish leaves and has a long succession of soft, light yellow flowers, on 4 in. stems. Seed is the only means of reproduction of both the above, and they often self-sow.

Parahebe ○
(Scrophulariaceae)

This name has now been given to some sub-shrubby hebes, all of which formerly came under *Veronica P. catarractae*. These make low mounds of dark green shiny leaves and pale lilac flowers in early summer, growing to 10 in. The form 'Diffusus' is dwarfed at 6 in. and more desirable. *P. lyallii* is more upright at 6-8 in. with near-white flowers, and 'Miss Willmott' is of similar height with pinkish-lilac flowers. The taller ones respond to trimming with shears after flowering, but *P. bidwillii* is too small to need this, being only 2 in. of bronzy leaves and a few white flowers. Parahebes can be divided and combine agreeably with most penstemons.

Penstemon ○
(Scrophulariaceae)

This varied genus includes both dwarf herbaceous and some shrubby species. The latter especially need a sunny place and sharp drainage. *P. alpinus* forms clumps of broad leaves and has 8 in. spikes of light blue flowers in May to June. *P. barrattae* is of similar height with blue-purple tubular flowers and *P. virens* has small but intensely deep blue flowers on 6 in. spikes above green-leaved mats. These three are non-shrubby and can be divided or reared from seed. The shrubby kinds may also come from seed but are better from cuttings after flowering. The erect growing *P. heterophyllus* 'Blue Gem' has very showy sky-blue spikes to 8 in. This comes only from seed. *P. edithae* has large purple-rose flowers on low 10 in. bushes. *P. pinifolius* grows erectly with narrow leaves and sprays of scarlet flowers to 8 in. *P. roezlii* is low growing at 6 in. with deep red flowers and effective in or on a wall. *P. scouleri* has light lavender flowers, growing to 8 in. and the cultivar 'Six Hills' has large, soft lilac flowers on 4-6 in. stems. Shrubby penstemons respond to top dressing with sandy soil in which new roots can form, but it is advisable to sometimes replant more deeply or take cuttings if they appear to be losing vigor. Several other species are in cultivation.

Penstemon pinifolius and Genista tinctoria 'Plena'

Penstemon edithae

Phlox subulata 'Blue Eyes'

Phlox douglasii

Phlox
(Polemoniaceae)

Phlox subulata 'Temiscaming'

The easiest and most popular kinds come under the species *P. douglasii* or *P. subulata,* both being groundcovers and capable of rooting as they spread.

They are invaluable for making a bright display in spring and early summer. They are especially effective on a slope, needing no special soil or attention, given good drainage and a mainly sunny position. Those under *P. douglasii* have a color range from white to lilac, pale blue and pink, with close-growing mats of small leaves and flowers and generally of neat habit. Height is 2 in. In *P. subulata* some brighter colors, including crimson red are available among the twenty or so cultivars in existence. Most of them have a quicker spread than *P. douglasii* and flower at about 3 in. high. Few alpine phlox need shade and peaty or acid soil, although *P. adsurgens* prefers such conditions: it has small leathery leaves and heads of soft pink flowers. This is not an easy plant, in contrast to *P. amoena* which is undemanding in a sunny position. Its growth is more tufted though still mat forming with magenta-pink flower heads, and there is also a pretty variegated-leaved form. *P. stolonifera* spreads quickly, with blue, pink or white flowers having self-rooting rosettes or runners with rounded leaves. It flowers in spring at 4 in. and is best in cool soil and some shade, as is *P. divaricata (P. canadensis). P. d. laphami* has loose heads of clear lavender-blue flowers in May to June. It prefers a soil enriched with peat or leaf-mold. All the above may be increased from cuttings.

Phyllitis ◑ ●
(Aspleniaceae)

P. scolopendrium is the well known Hart's-tongue fern. It is not out of place in a rocky wall with some shade, and the variations 'Cristata' and 'Undulata' (crested and wavy edged) are most attractive. They are not fussy as to soil and are long lived.

Phyllitis scolopendrium 'Undulata'

Phyteuma comosum

Phyteuma
(Campanulaceae)

They have distinctive blue flower heads with sharply pointed petals. The best known *P. comosum* is a good little plant, only 3 in., and happy in a crevice between rocks. It has lilac-blue flowers, as has the taller *P. orbiculare*, both being easy to grow. *P. scheuchzeri* has deep purple flowers on 8 in. stems. All flower in spring and early summer and are best perpetuated by seed.

Polemonium ○
(Polemoniaceae)

Only a few of the Jacob's ladders can be included. All have divided leaves (from which the folk name is derived) and sprays of small open cup-shaped flowers in early summer. *P. pauciflorum* has ferny leaves and pendulant, light yellow flowers, 6 in. tall. P. *reptans* is both vigorous and adaptable; best in the cultivar 'Blue Pearl', making a bright but rather brief display of blue flowers on 8 in. stems in May to June.

Polygala
(Polygalaceae)

The non-shrubby *P. calcarea* forms a tidy mat of dark green covered with brilliant blue flowers, 2 in. high in early summer. It is a good scree plant for limy soils, sometimes reproducing itself from seed. In contrast, two other somewhat shrubby species are strictly for acid peaty soil. *P. chamaebuxus* is a low evergreen bush 5 in. high. In this type the pea-shaped flowers are cream and yellow, but P. c. 'Purpurea' are maroon and yellow, while in P. c. 'Grandiflora' they are deep pink and gold. They flower from April to June and though not adaptable, make a good display where suited. *P. vayredae* is not spectacular, having narrow foliage to 6 in. and small purplish flowers. They look fine in association with erythroniums.

Polemonium

Polygonatum falcatum

Polygonatum ◑ ●
(Liliaceae)

The taller Solomon's seals are best in shade and this applies also to two dwarf species. *P. falcatum* has short leafy stems and sprays of tiny white flowers 6 in. tall in spring from creeping shoots just below surface. *P. hookeri* also forms mats of greenery in summer, but is smaller and has minute spikes of rosy-lilac flowers. Both prefer a cool or peaty soil which does not dry out. Division in autumn.

Polygonum
(Polygonaceae)

This large genus is immensely varied in form and requirements. Some are weedy but those below are good garden plants. *P. affine* is variable and is best for giving both flowers and groundcover, but should be kept away from slow growing plants. The pink poker-like spikes are up to 8 in. tall. *P. a.* 'Donald Lowndes' is a good free-flowering form and 'Darjeeling Red' has thinner, deep rose spikes. These are of rapid surface-rooting growth and sometimes die out in patches, needing replanting. They flower at intervals during the summer and autumn. *P. tenuicaule* is spring flowering with little 4 in. spikes of white from a clumpy plant, best in moist soil. *P. vaccinifolium* is a splendid late flowering species and although a little invasive it is easily curbed. The congested twiggy mat covers itself with slender spikes of bright rose pink in sun or shade, 4 in. high. It is, however, more at home in non-limy soil. Where scope permits, the newly discovered is worth having. *P. amplexicaule* 'Arun Gem' has dangling pokers of bright pink and a neat habit. Although 12-16 in. tall, it is charmingly graceful and flowers from July till cut back to a compact root by frost. It grows in any good soil in sun or partial shade and can be divided.

Polygonum amplexicaule 'Arun Gem'

Polygonum affine 'Donald Lowndes'   *Polygonum vaccinifolium*

84

Potentilla
(Rosaceae)

These showy, easily grown plants will succeed in any reasonable soil and, while preferring sun, do not object to some partial shade. The popular shrubby kinds are too large for most rock gardens but the same open-petalled flowers in similar colors are represented on the dwarfer types of tufted, clumpy or mat-forming habit. All are easy to divide when they become old and less free to flower. *P. aurea* forms green prostrate mats with ample golden flowers in summer and there is a double flowered form of this. Both grow 2 in. tall. *P. alba* is white, more tufted and 6 in. tall. *P. eriocarpa* is mat forming, with grey-green foliage and light yellow flowers for most of the summer, and *P. tommasiniana (P. cinerea)* quickly forms a grey-silver mat with a show of yellow in spring. The silver-leaved tufts of *P. nitida* have rose-pink flowers 2 in. tall in early summer and the tiny, green-leaved *tabernaemontani (verna nana)* has yellow flowers for most of the summer. *P. ternata (chrysocraspeda)* has larger green tufts and yellow flowers for many weeks, but *P. t. aurantiaca* is orange buff. Both are 3 in. tall. *P. t. tonguei* is outstanding for its prostrate sprays of crimson-blotched, light orange flowers from June till autumn. To round off the list, *P. fragiformis (P. megalantha)* has bright yellow flowers above silky, silvery foliage in early summer at 8 in.

Potentilla ternata tonguei

Potentilla aurea

Pratia ◑
(Campanulaceae)

P. treadwellii forms prostrate mats and has stemless white flowers followed by purple berries. It prefers a cool, semi-shaded place where not dry or exposed. Divide in spring.

Primula denticulata

Primula rosea 'Delight'

Primula
(Primulaceae)

This vast genus is best divided into groups, not all of which are within the scope of this book. Most tall 'Bog' primulas and the more difficult woodland or 'Petiolares' types must be excluded. The alpine *auricula* is attractive in sun or part shade having leathery, sometimes 'mealy or powdered' leaves. Heads of flowers are purple, blue, white, yellow and near red. These grow in most well drained soils but occasionally need to be divided or replanted more deeply. There are many under this general heading needing a mainly sunny place, good soil and drainage but they are also suitable for troughs and an alpine house. The 'Primrose' types will also grow in ordinary soil in sun or part shade where not too dry and there, if not 'alpine' in the strict sense (except for a few very small species as distinct from cultivars), they make a bright display in spring. These remarks could also apply to the popular *P. denticulata* with rounded heads of white, mauve, violet and pink which make a spring display, reaching 10 in. and disliking dry soil. Another bright moisture-loving species is *P. rosea*, the flower clusters rising in early spring before the leaves, intensely deep pink in *P. r.* 'Delight', to reach 8 in. in May. All these are easy to grow in leafy or peaty soil and shade. The woodland primulas are more difficult to please and keep alive in dry climates, where they may need renewal from seed after two to three years. They include the pretty *P. capitata*, with powdered globular heads, 6 in. tall, and the white-flowered *P. chionantha*, 12 in., with leathery leaves. *P. frondosa* is a dainty lilac at 5 in.; *nutans*, purple, 4 in.; *polyneura*, magenta, 8 in.; *yargongensis (wardii)*, pale lilac, 6 in. and the bright orange *P. cockburniana*.

P. sieboldii is more reliably perennial. This forms a slow creeping mat just below the surface. Flowers and leaves come up together in April to form a charming picture. The type is pale pink, but the clearer pink 'Geisha Girl' is better and there is a magenta-pink 'Mikado'. The white 'Snowflakes' is very beautiful indeed, combining delightfully with *Trillium sessile* and *Corydalis cashmeriana*. These *sieboldii* primulas, being shallow rooted, benefit from a peaty top dressing in late summer.

Other reliable primulas for peaty or moist soil include *P. secundiflora*, deep crimson, at 12 in.; *P. alpicola* producing white, lemon or lavender drooping heads, May to July, and also the relatively later flowering *P. sikkimensis* which has sweetly scented yellow bells on 14 in. stems. The above is a fairly modest selection for the genus *Primula*, which attracts many enthusiastic collectors, who can indulge themselves in hundreds of species and cultivars if they wish.

Primula sieboldii 'Snowflakes'

Primula marginata

Prunella
(Labiatae)

These are among the easiest plants to grow, having mat-forming roots, ample leafage and a profusion of short spikes in summer. There are many variations of *P. incisa*, which has deeply cut, dark green leaves and magenta flowers from June to July. *P. incisa* 'Rubra' is more of a reddish purple, as is *P. webbiana*, but the most colorful is 'Rotkappchen' ('Little Red Riding Hood') with flowers of deep carmine red. All the above flower from June to August at 5-6 in. but *P. x* 'Loveliness' in white, pink and lilac shades is taller at 10 in. All are best cut back hard after flowering.

Pterocephalus ○
(Dipsaceae)

P. parnassi forms cushions of soft open grey foliage, studded with stemless, pink, scabious-type flowers which appear on and off during summer. It is best in fairly dry soil and makes a good wall plant. Divide in spring.

Prunella webbiana

Pulsatilla ○
(Ranunculaceae)

P. vulgaris (Anemone pulsatilla) is a long lived plant for a sunny position in well drained soil. It is fairly adaptable as to soil but is best where there is lime. The buds are almost cocooned as they emerge in March, before the ferny, greyish foliage, but open out into goblet form, with prominent orange-yellow stamens. Colors vary and may be obtained in white, pale pink, shades of lilac and lavender to maroon and red. In cultivation they sometimes attain 12 in. as flowering fades but are generally about 8 in. The fluffy seedheads are attractive for much of the summer. It can only be reproduced from seed, best sown as soon as ripe.

Pulsatilla vulgaris 'Rubra'

Ramonda ◑
(Gesneriaceae)

Ranunculus montanus

Ramonda myconi

These charming plants make dark green rosettes up to 5 in. across of deep green, crinkled leaves. In spring and early summer they produce 4 in., stems carrying lavender-mauve, golden-centered flowers. They naturally grow in rock crevices facing away from the sun and are best so planted rather than on the flat. *R. myconi* and the rarer *R. nathaliae* do not greatly differ and though both are long lived, they are best reproduced from seed.

Ranunculus gramineus

Ranunculus
(Ranunculaceae)

This genus includes a few good garden plants as well as the weedy buttercups. They are not fussy as to soil, but dislike dry positions. All flower in spring and early summer. *R. amplexicaulis*, best in the form *grandiflora*, has narrow glaucous foliage from a small, fleshy rooted plant and produces sprays carrying a few, but quite large, open pure white flowers in spring at 6-8 in., dying back to dormancy by August. *R. gouanii* makes a neat green clump, bright with golden flowers in May to June at 5 in. *R. gramineus* is distinct for its grassy, grey-green leaves and stems. It carries a bright display of shining yellow flowers on 10 in. sprays from May to July. *R. montanus* has a long dormant period but covers itself with burnished gold blooms in May, only 4 in. high in the cultivar 'Molten Gold'. *R. bulbosus* (*R. speciosus*) is best in the double form 'Plenus' with very large flowers of glistening yellow, tinged green. Growing to 10 in., it likes moisture and makes a leafy clump of greenery after flowering in May-June. All these ranunculus may be safely divided in early autumn.

Raoulia ○
(Compositae)

These form close, surface-rooting mats, almost like a film, and are of reasonably quick spread. They are best in sandy soil and full sun. Although they may die out in patches during severe winters, they are easily replaced in spring. *R. australis* is the best known for its tight mats of tiny, silvery rosettes. The small, buff-colored flowers only 1/2 in. high are of no consequence and this applies to the slightly larger and even more silvery *R. hookeri. R. lutescens* and *R. tenuicaulis* are of more rapid growth and quite good for paving and carpeting, with minute yellowish flowers. All are easily divided and have no deep roots.

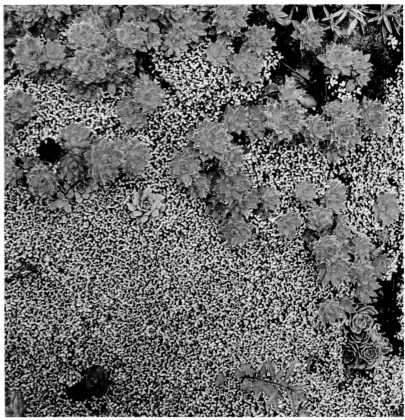

Raoulia australis

Rhodohypoxis baurii

Rhodohypoxis ○
(Hypoxidaceae)

These South African plants are only suitable for warm sheltered positions, or for troughs and pans under glass. They are best dried off in winter and should not be deprived of moisture in summer. The species *R. baurii* is variable, but may be obtained true to color in named cultivars from white through pink to red and although only 2 in. when in flower, it continues to grow from May till late summer. Where happy, clumps are best divided when renewed growth begins in April.

The owners of this garden have followed their own fancies by mixing alpines with taller subjects. Although pleasing and to a non-purist quite interesting, there will soon be harmful competition between the tall, vigorous plants, and the more choice, slower growing alpines.

The grassy clump is the pretty Molinia caerulea 'Variegata' which dies down in winter just as does the starry-flowered campanula on the left.

Sanguinaria
(Papaveraceae)

The American bloodroot *(S. canadensis),* is so called because of the color of sap in its fleshy roots. These are brittle but will divide with care. The double *S. c.* 'Plena' is the most desirable form with large pure white flowers at 6 in. quickly followed by lobed, glaucous foliage. Its fault is in its brief display in spring, but it is, none the less, prized as a rarity for good light or peaty soil not liable to dry out. Division after flowering or in late winter.

Saponaria 'Bressingham'

Saponaria
(Caryophyllaceae)

These have open flowers shaped like dianthus in shades of pink and rosy red. *S. caespitosa* makes a close green hummock set with magenta-pink flowers in spring. It needs well drained soil, as does the deep-rooted *S. olivana* which is a little taller at 2 in. A tufty clump, it produces light pink flowers from May to July. The best known is the quicker growing trailer *S. ocymoides*. This makes a trailing mound well covered with deep rose-pink flowers from May to August at 6 in. The choicest is a cross between the last two, *S.* 'Bressingham'. This is slow to make a low mound with a display of near-red flowers and is only 2 in. It is best in scree soil, not too dry and happy in part shade. Only *S. ocymoides* comes freely from seed, the others being increased by basal cuttings.

Saponaria ocymoides

Satureia
(Labiatae)

These have small flowers and mostly aromatic foliage. Valuable for being autumn flowering. *S. montana* makes a fairly large mound to 10 in. with bright blue flowers in autumn in the form 'Caerulea'. *S. repanda* makes considerable summer spread of trailing growth, useful for walls with its white flowers. Both can be divided in spring.

Saxifraga
(Saxifragaceae)

Group 1
Group 2
Group 3
Group 4

Saxifraga aizoides atrorubens

Saxifraga apiculata

This large and diverse genus is also best divided into groups in keeping with cultural requirements based on natural habitat. The easiest to grow in ordinary soil other than in hot dry positions are the 'mossy' saxifrages, Group 1. These have green rosettes forming a low mound or carpet, almost invariably green and having sprays of open, bell-shaped flowers in April to May. Colors obtainable vary from white to cream, many shades of pink through to blood red and vary in height from 2-8 in. in named cultivars. They are best replanted every two to three years to restore neatness and vigor.

Group 2 has similar cultural requirements and includes the ubiquitous London pride *S. umbrosa* (now *S. urbium*) which is valuable for shady places giving good evergreen groundcover and a show of small, deep pink flowers on 10 in. stems. This has dwarfed cultivars, such as *primuloides* 'Elliott's Variety', a neat miniature with evergreen rosettes and flowers 4 in. high. The white *S. cuneifolia* is pretty and there is one form with variegated rosettes. *S. aizoides atrorubens* is a slow growing, green groundcover having brownish-red flowers in summer at 2 in. A cross between this and *S. primuloides*, named 'Primulaize' is charming for its 3 in. sprays of deep carmine from June to September. This is best in shade and peaty soil, as is the handsome *S. fortunei* and its variations.

These are shallow rooting, clump-forming plants and make a fine canopy of large, handsome leaves from spring till October when they erupt into showers of starry-white flowers to 10 in. The type is green leaved, coppery green underneath but 'Wada's Variety' has reddish-purple leaves, while *rubrifolia* is coppery red. The last two have flowers above the leaves about 8 in. tall. Although not 100 percent hardy in cold areas, they are easily protected with leaves from November to March to insure survival. They appreciate a spring application of a peaty top dressing. In this group must be placed the early flowering *S. oppositifolia*. They prefer some sun, provided moisture is not lacking. They form mats of dark, sessile foliage and the terminal flowers are little cups of intensely bright pink, only 1 in. above ground in March to April. They root down as they spread and are quite evergreen. Replanting is best in early summer when moist.

Group 3 is of cushion-forming saxifrages, known as Kabschias. With a few exceptions, these are slow growing and although they need well drained soil, many preferring sandy or scree conditions, they dislike being in full

Saxifraga oppositifolia

Saxifraga fortunei rubrifolia

Saxifraga umbrosa primuloides 'Elliott's Variety'

sun all day. The easier, faster growing kinds have sizable low mounds of mostly green or grey-green rosettes with flowers in white or yellow shades showing color often by March and continuing through April. They grow 2-4 in. tall. *S. apiculata* is the best known with primrose-yellow flowers and a white form 'Alba'. *S. haagii* and 'Gold Dust' are deeper yellow and 'Elizabethae' soft yellow. There are very many Kabschias in the slower growing range, most of them being silver-leaved cultivars, having white, pink and near-red flowers as well as shades of yellow. The tiny, close-packed rosettes are hard to the touch, some with stemless flowers, which are virtually at ground level. Others have short stems 4-5 in. tall as clustered flower spikes. The range includes choice connoisseurs' items which are grown in scree soil, troughs or in an alpine house. The best known of proven worth are *burserana* 'Gloria' for a white; 'Cranbourne' and 'Jenkinsae' for light pink; 'Megasaeflora' and 'Bridget' for deep pink; 'Grace Farwell' or 'Winifred' for a near red; 'Faldonside', lemon yellow, and 'Valerie Finnis', primrose yellow. All flower February to April.

Group 4 is of 'encrusted' or Aizoon

Saxifraga lingulata

Saxifraga graminifolia 'Pinkushion'

saxifrages. These make rosettes mostly silvered, varying in size from under 1/2 in. diameter to 8 in. or more with long, radiating leaves. The smaller ones are cushion forming, for gritty but not poor or very dry soil. They like lime as do most saxifrages, and in the wild are often found growing in chinks and crevices in limestone mountain regions. The largest *S. longifolia* grows only in the Pyrenees in mainly vertical positions. The Aizoons are easier to grow outdoors than the more precocious Englerias. Flower spikes arise from the center of mature rosettes and are usually in spray formation with a large number of small individual flowers in white (some spotted pink) and various shades of pink. A few are light yellow, such as the green-rosette *S. aizoon* 'Lutea' and the cultivar 'Esther'. Both are 8-10 in. tall and generally this group flowers in May and June. Whites predominate, from the tiny *S. cochlearis* 'Minor' at 4 in. to the magnificent 'Tumbling Waters' at 24 in. from a huge rosette. In between is the pretty 'Southside Seedling' with spotted flowers at 12 in., 'Dr. Ramsey', 8 in. white and 'Kathleen Pinsent', shell pink, 6 in. tall. All these saxifrages are best from cuttings of individual rosettes taken after flowering.

S. graminifolia is not only very long lived but has a wealth of narrow basal foliage of silvery hue, making a broad mound 6 in. high, just above which come lavender-blue flowers from June to September. There is a pretty pink-flowered cultivar named 'Pinkushion' and both are very good plants, dividable in spring.

Scabiosa ○
(Dipsaceae)

Both species below are dwarf and mounded with the typical pincushion-type flowers over a long period. *S. alpina,* however, is not very long lived, though it reproduces easily from seed and old plants will rejuvenate by division. The light blue flowers come on 5 in. stems held erectly above the green tufted plants.

Scleranthus ○
(Caryophyllaceae)

S. biflorus is grown for its unusually tight mounded cushions of distinctly golden hue. The tiny yellow flowers are of little note, but it is a very effective plant for trough or alpine house.

95

Scutellaria ○
(Labiatae)

Known as skull cap, from the shape of the flower, these bloom after the spring flush of alpines. *S. alpina* makes a surface mat of saw-edged leaves and has 4 in. spikes of pretty cream and purple bicolor flowers from July to September. *S. hastata* grows erectly with lavender-blue flowers on 5 in. spikes in June to July, but is inclined to be invasive, as is the deeper blue *S. scordiifolia* of similar height. The choicest, for scree or alpine house is *S. indica japonica*, which makes a mound of soft grey-green foliage and has a succession of deep lavender-blue flowers at 5 in. from June to October. All the above are easy to divide in spring.

Scutellaria scordiifolia

Sedum
(Crassulaceae)

The name stonecrop strictly applies to one species *S. acre*, which, with a few others such as *S. album* and *S. dasyphyllum*, should be avoided for being a nuisance among choicer plants, although *S. album murale* is useful as a wall plant. Many sedums are evergreen groundcovers, rooting as they spread, and with very few exceptions all are very easy to grow in well drained soil and sun. Some like the true stonecrop, needs virtually no soil at all.

Others form clumpy growth, dying back in winter after a show of yellow, pink or red flowers. *S. ewersit* has near-prostrate growth with glaucous foliage and heads of pink flowers in July to August at 6 in. 'Weihenstephaner Gold' makes a fine show from June onwards above dense green leaves. *S. middendorffianum* is also deep yellow and neater growing at 4 in. as is the purple-green-leaved *S. oreganum (obtusatum)* at 3 in. The powdery grey-purple mounded forms of *S. spathulifolium* grow only to 2 in., flowering in June to July. *S. spurium* makes spreading carpets with no nuisance value and has heads of glistening pink to red flowers June to August at 3

Sedum 'Vera Jameson'

in. All make good foliage foil and in some, notably 'Purple Carpet' and 'Ruby Mantle' the leaves themselves are purple-maroon in color, attractive almost the year round. The cultivar named 'Green Mantle' does not flower but makes a close evergreen, trouble free carpet through which bulbs and some dwarf shrubs can grow.

Among the smaller growing sedums which die back in the winter to a compact rootstock are some that make a charming display in late summer at about 3 in. tall. These are *S. lidakense* and *S. pluricaule* and *S. cauticolum*. The latter is a lighter pink. Hybrid cultivars from this are a little taller. 'Ruby Glow' is very showy at 6 in. and

Sedum album murale

Sedum spurium 'Erdblut'

Sedum spathulifolium

'Vera Jameson' is of similar height with glistening, deep pink heads. Both flower July to September. *S. tatarinowii* is a more compact and upright species with flesh-pink flower heads.

Most iceplant-type sedums are too tall for rock gardens, at 12-16 in., though they make a splendid autumn display. There are, however, a few with glaucous succulent foliage and fleshy roots which flower in spring and are not too tall. *S. rhodiola (R. rosea)* and *S. heterodontum (Rhodiola rosea heterodontum)* both very attractive and long lived, are about 10 in. tall. *S. fastigiatum* has rich green foliage like pine needles from 6-8 in. upright stems, which open to a rusty-brown flower head in summer.

The plants above are a selection from the best of this large genus, most of which are so easy to grow that they can be moved or divided for replanting at almost any time of the year.

Sedum rhodiola

Sempervivum ○
(Crassulaceae)

Of all alpine plants these could be said to have the least need of good soil. The name houseleek applies to a species *S. tectorum*, after it was seen growing on tiled roofs. It is said to have some value against lightning damage. All form rosettes, which expand as others begin to grow from beneath the lower layer of fleshy leaves. They are fascinating plants to grow and are very adaptable to pot or pan culture as well as to many other positions where soil is well drained. They will grow quite well in old ashes and rubble; the best colorings come when grown in semi-arid soils. In richer, moister soils they are apt to grow too lush and lose color, as well as compactness. The smallest are those with 'spider web' filaments in the rosette from which the specific name *arachnoideum* is derived. It has silver-grey rosettes ¹/₂ in. in diameter and deep pink flowers on 1¹/₂ in. stems. Sempervivums, that do flower, bloom in early summer. But only in a few varieties do these flowers add to their attraction. Sometimes the flowering rosettes die out afterwards, but the gap is usually filled by new ones. Two

Sempervivum arachnoideum laggeri   *Sempervivum* 'Mahogany'

good and slightly larger forms of *S. arachnoideum* are seen in *S. a. laggeri*, *S. giuseppi* and 'Jubilee', all pink flowered. Those with small rosettes in silver, green or tinged purple will fill crevices very neatly or a low hummock gradually expands where space permits. They can be left to themselves for years to give year round interest, as do all sempervivums.

Sempervivum arachnoideum

Sempervivum ornatum

Those with more colorful rosettes in shades of green towards mahogany, bronzy purple and crimson, are legion. In total, sempervivums run into several hundreds, each differing in some respect and thereby making them attractive to collectors who lack the means or the will for intensive, challenging cultivations as needed with many choice, temperamental alpines. A few of the larger growing, colorful species and cultivars such as 'Alpha', 'Beta', 'Commander Hay', 'Mahogany', 'Othello', 'Rubin', *marmoreum rubrifolium*, 'Triste' and 'Noir' can be recommended, but in recent years a host of new varieties have arrived from plant breeders to widen still more the range available.

A giant among the wide variations of sempervivums is surrounded by the neat growing, yellow Sedum middendorffianum.

Serratula
(Compositae)

S. seoanei (erroneously called *shawii),* although a little tall at 10 in., is included because of its late flowering and easy culture. It has deep green, fingered foliage. In September and October it carries a display of purple-rose flower heads on erect stems. These are fluffy, thistle-like but there are no prickles.

Silene schafta

Silene ○
(Caryophyllaceae)

These are generally easy to grow plants in any well drained soil although *S. acaulis* may be seen growing where quite damp in the wild. The best in this close mat-forming species is *S. a. pedunculata* with a display in spring and early summer of small, clear pink flowers. *S. alpestris* forms deep green tufts and sends up 8 in. sprays of white flowers, which in the double form 'Plena' are much more effective for early summer display. *S. maritima* is also available in a double white form 'Plena' as well as the single, and in the pale pink 'Rosea'. This makes compact, glaucous-leaved plants and has prostrate sprays of quite large flowers in summer 1 in. or more across. This type is especially good for walls, but *S. schafta* makes very little spread and forms a neat, green-leaved plant with 6 in. spikes of bright pink from July to September. The more vigorous and reliable *S. s.* 'Robusta' has larger flowers from a steadily expanding plant flowering continuously from July to October, in a similar color and height. These are all quite reliable plants, dividable in spring but *S. schafta* comes best from seed. These associate agreeably with campanulas.

Sisyrinchium bermudianum

Sisyrinchium ○
(Iridaceae)

These too are very easy to grow with a long flowering season. In habit they resemble miniature grassy-leaved iris but in flower they are simple and open, making up for lack of size in numbers produced. *S. bellum* and *S. bermudianum* have deep blue flowers on 6 in. stems from early June to August. *S. angustifolia* is narrow leaved, with light violet flowers on 8 in. stems with 'Blue Star' a very free-flowering cultivar. *S. brachypus* and *S. californicum* are both yellow at 6 in. but the latter is less hardy. There is a white form of *S. bellum* and a white-flowering cultivar named 'Mrs. Spiney'. All the above have compact tufty growth and as each little fan has its own roots, division is very simple.

Soldanella ◑ ●
(Primulaceae)

These charming spring flowering
plants sometimes baffle would-be cul-
tivators. They demand well drained,
but not dry, sandy soil rich in humus,
and shade, preferably not under trees.
They form spreading clumps where
happy, with a low canopy of deep
green, circular leaves and dainty, lace-
edged flowers dangling from slender
stalks. *S. alpina* is lavender blue spotted crimson only 2½ in. high but not
so free to flower as *S. montana villosa*.
This has a more vigorous spread and
ample rounded foliage beneath 4 in.
lavender-blue flowers. *S. pindicola* has
more heart-shaped leaves with lilac-
lavender flowers on 5 in. stems. *S.
minima* is similar but only 3 in. tall.
Division is best in early autumn or
early spring, and older plants benefit
from a little top dressing to assist their
shallow rooting system. They look effective with early primulas.

Soldanella montana villosa

Solidago x 'Golden Thumb'

Solidago ○
(Compositae)

As golden rod these are considered tall
border plants, but three are sufficiently dwarf to include here. One is the
species *S. brachystachys* which sends
up 8 in. spikes of deep yellow in late
summer from a compact clumpy plant.
S. x 'Golden Thumb' and the similar
'Queenie', have golden-green foliage
up until August or September when it
opens out into a broad plume of gold-
en yellow at 10 in. A seldom seen
early flowering species exists in *S. vir-
gaurea nana*, which has congested
spikes of deep yellow in June to July,
only 6 in. tall.

Several helianthemum flowers stand out against the violet-blue of the veronica. The effect is further enhanced by a magnificent clump of white dianthus and the pale pink gypsophila. Dwarf conifers provide contrast in shape and texture.

Stachys nivea

Stachys ○
(Labiatae)

S. nivea forms neat evergreen clumps close to the surface of deep green, crinkled leaves. From June to late summer, come 6 in. erect poker-like spikes of pure white. An easy and useful plant which adds to variety and enhances other late flowering plants such as sedums.

Synthyris ◗ ●
(Scrophulariaceae)

S. reniformis makes a neat mound of deep green, saw-edged leaves, and has bright blue flowers on 4 in. sprays in April and May. This is a slow growing plant for a cool shady place having rarity value. Division is best after flowering.

Thalictrum kiusianum

Tanacetum ○
(Compositae)

Two silver-leaved species (sometimes listed as *Chrysanthemum*) for sun and well drained soil. *T. densum* 'Amani' has a vigorous spread above ground, with fine silvery filigree foliage, but a sparce show of small yellow flowers on 6 in. stems. This is an excellent groundcover but has a tendency to die out in patches after winter, though this is easily remedied by replanting young rooted pieces in spring. *T. herderi* is a splendid little silvery plant. It is compact growing and has yellow button flowers to 8 in. in summer. Division best in spring.

Tanakea ◗ ●
(Saxifragaceae)

T. radicans has a similar requirement and forms a carpet of pretty greenery 3 in. high above which come tiny flowered sprays of creamy-white flowers, tinged green, in summer. It spreads slowly from runners and can be divided in spring.

Teucrium ○
(Labiatae)

These are not spectacular but some add variety to the rather sparce range of later flowering alpines. *T. ackermanii* has short clustered spikes of deep red on greyish mounds and both *T. aureum (polium)* and *aroanium* form silvery mounds with insignificant flowers. All three are about 4 in. high, but *T. subspinosum* is only 2 in. in a tight hummock of spiny silvery foliage set with minute pink flowers. This is late flowering and all are best in light soil. *T. chamaedrys nanum* makes a compact, shrubby evergreen bush of deep green with 10 in. spikes of deep pink in late summer. Easy in any soil.

Thalictrum ◗ ●
(Ranunculaceae)

A genus varying in height from under 2 in. to 8 in. The smallest, *T. kiusianum*, is a first class species given well drained, but not dry, peaty or humus-rich soil and shade. The roots are very small and shallow but capable of spreading to form a loose mat of pretty leaves of purple green through which comes a long display of fluffy lilac flowers only 2 in. high from June to autumn. Old plants fall apart for replanting, best done in spring. *T. coreanum* is a little larger in all its parts, and is clump-forming with lilac 'powder-puff' flowers on 4 in. stems.

Thymus ○
(Labiatae)

These include some indispensables, both as groundcovers and erect growing kinds. Many have aromatic foliage. The true lemon-scented *T. citriodorus* is bush-forming at 6 in. but the green-leaved type is unworthy when there are both gold, 'Aureus', and silver, 'Silver Queen', 'Silver Posie' or variegated forms. Flowering is not conspicuous. There are also creeping mat-like thymes with colorful, scented leaves named 'Golden Dwarf' and 'Doone Valley', the latter being deep green, speckled with gold in the mass.

The closer creeping thymes include the May to June flowering grey-leaved *T. praecox (T. doerfleri)* of which the cultivar 'Bressingham Seedling' is extra good. They flower at only 2 in., as do the most colorful variations of *T. drucei,* (formerly *T. serpyllum*). A firm favorite is *T.d.* 'Coccineus' with masses of near-red flowers June to July and *T.d.* 'Major', a little paler but larger. The cultivars 'Annie Hall', flesh pink, 'Snowdrift' or 'Albus', white and 'Pink Chintz', clear pink, complete the color range. The form 'Minus' is a mere film of green with pink flowers at 1 in. and *lanuginosus* has a grey woolly appearance. All these are excellent paving plants and do not object to being trodden upon. The smaller forms of *T. drucei* will allow bulbs to come through their mats. If trodden on or bruised *T. herbabarona* gives off a strong caraway-like scent from its deep green foliage. This, too, has a creeping habit, as has *T. montanus,* a vigorous green species, very free with its 2³/₄ in. heads of pink from July to August.

A few thymes are not fully hardy in cold districts, and *T. cilicicus, ericifolius (Micromeria varia), membranaceus and micans (caespititius)* are best grown in scree or an alpine house. All are low mounded and sub-shrubby, but the hardier sub-shrubby kinds are well worth growing. The name 'E.B. Anderson' has been given to a low

Thymus praecox 'Bressingham Seedling'

Thymus 'Doone Valley'

Thymus drucei 'Coccineus'

Thymus 'E.B. Anderson'

mounded type, (correctly known as *Acinos alpinus meridionalis*), with deep green leaves and a long display of lavender-mauve flowers at 3 in. *Thymus nitidus* is more shrubby, quite erect at 8 in. and grey leaved. It has clear pink flowers from June to July, and there are very good forms in the more compact 'Peter Davis' and 'Valerie Finnis'. Of similar growth but with almost too vigorous a spread for small gardens is the bright pink 8 in. 'Porlock', flowering in May to June. All thymes are best divided after flowering where not dry, or in early spring.

Tiarella ◑ ●
(Saxifragaceae)

Tiarella cordifolia

These are shade-loving plants giving excellent groundcover where soils are not too dry, heavy or with a high lime content. The best known is *T. cordifolia*, which spreads from runners having ivy-shaped, light green leaves and a delightful display of 6 in. dainty white flower sprays in May to June. *T. collina* is of more clumpy growth, and because of abundant leafage is always attractive. In May to July it sends up a profusion of 10 in. pearly-white flowers. Both of these are easy to divide in early autumn but *T. wherryi* comes best from seed. It is not always long lived, but is, however, very long flowering with 10 in. creamy-white sprays from slightly golden-green foliage. *T. polyphylla* and *T. trifoliata* are also long flowering and with good foliage cover all year. White flowers are borne on 6 in. stems.

Townsendia ○
(Compositae)

This charming midget blue daisy, *T. formosana*, is best in scree soil and good for troughs. It has wide-rayed flowers with yellow centers 2 in. high. Unfortunately, it is short lived, but is easily reproduced from seed.

Tunica ○
(Caryophyllaceae)

Dainty little plants, allied to *Gypsophila*, and very useful for late flowering. The single flowered pink species, *T. saxifraga*, is rather short lived but comes easily from seed, to give a display of small, open pink flowers, above narrow leaves, from July onwards. Much more showy and choice, for sandy soil, is a double white 'Alba Plena' and the double pink 'Rosette', which can be divided in spring. All are about 6 in. in height.

Trollius
(Ranunculaceae)

Unlike the taller globe flowers the dwarf kinds are flat-petalled but very bright. *T. acaulis* needs well drained, but not dry soil, with peat and has wide, glistening golden flowers on erect 8 in. stems. *T. pumilus*, best in 'Wargrave Variety' is a little taller and more vigorous for moist soil. Both flower in early summer and can be divided after flowering.

Valeriana
(Valerianaceae)

The species *V. montana* and *V. saxatilis* both form green, vigorous mats and give a rather brief display of shell-pink heads in early summer, at about 6 in. They can be divided after flowering, and are easy, adaptable plants, except for hot, dry conditions.

Tunica 'Rosette'   *Valeriana montana*

A varied collection of alpine plants has been skillfully positioned to enhance a flat area, only broken by a low wall. The use of rocks has been reduced to a minimum. It is an excellent example of the pleasing result obtainable on such a site.

Veronica
(Scrophulariaceae)

This large and varied genus has now lost its shrubby and sub-shrubby members to *Hebe* and *Parahebe* respectively. Few of those left as *Veronica* are evergreen but included are some very worthwhile, relatively easy to grow plants, most of which prefer sun to shade, though they are fairly adaptable. All are spike forming with small flowers in profusion close to the stem. *V. cinerea* has more or less year round grey leaves of mat-forming habit on which come light blue flowers on 6 in. spikes in early summer. *V. gentianoides* as a type is too tall, but the 8 in. *V. g.* 'Nana' is effective in May and June with its pale blue spikes above green tufts. *V. incana* is silvery leaved, close to the ground, and the 8 in. spikes in June to July are violet blue for good contrast. *V. prostrata (rupestris)* is rich blue on short 4 in. spikes and makes a real splash of color in May and June, as do the deeper, less vigorous 'Loddon Blue', the pink 'Mrs. Holt', while 'Blue Sheen' is light china blue. All are under 4 in. and mat forming. *V. pectinata* 'Rosea', pink, makes vigorous mats of soft grey-green foliage and has pink 'bird's eye' flowers. *V. whitleyi* is similar but with light blue flowers.

V. pinnata 'Blue Eyes' is a charming, upright growing plant with sky-blue flowers in May-June to 8 in. from a compact clump while *V. saturejoides* has green mats and deep blue flowers 3 in. tall from May to June. *V. spicata* has green-leaved, ground-hugging mats and erect blue spikes in June and July. Some variations of this are too tall, but *V. s. selleri* or 'Nana' are only 4 in. on very tight mats. There is a pretty white cultivar in *V.* 'Snow White' at 10 in. and a deep pink in 'Heidi'. 'Minuet' is grey leaved in

Veronica prostrata 'Blue Sheen'

Veronica pectinata 'Rosea'

Veronica cinerea

clear light pink 12 in. tall but the richest colors are seen in the 14 in. 'Blue Fox' and 'Red Fox'.

V. austriaca teucrium is best in its cultivars, though very few are sufficiently dwarf and compact. They make clumpy, deciduous plants, but for brilliance have few equals, flowering mainly in June. *V.* 'Kapitan' grows to 10 in. in massed spikes of gentian blue, 'Shirley Blue', 8 in. and 'Crater Lake Blue', 12 in. are a little later, and equally attractive. *V. a. t.* 'Trehane' has golden-green foliage and deep blue spikes. This prefers a little shade and rich, light soil. All the above are best divided and replanted every few years, which can be done in late summer or early spring. Although many others exist, these are a selection of the best.

Veronica prostrata

Viola
(Violaceae)

These well-loved plants may not be considered truly alpine, but some are well worth including. *V. cornuta* is quite a spreader, but has a long succession of light blue 'horned' pansy flowers, seen also in the white 'Alba' and the deep blue 'Purpurea'. All are 4-in., blooming May to August. In this category, but with more compact growth, are the cultivars 'Nora Leigh', light blue, 'Blue Carpet' and the yellow and maroon 'Jackanapes', all long flowering, growing 6 in. tall. *V. cucullata* is more on the style of a violet (*V. odorata*) but does not run. The white flowers, 6 in. high, have a violet-blue streak in *V. c. striata* as has *V. septentrionalis*. Both are at home where cool

and shady. This applies to the very good species *V. labradorica*, which has purplish rounded leaves giving excellent groundcover, even where dry, and lilac-mauve flowers bloom on 4 in. stems for a long period. *V. hederacea* is not fully hardy, though pretty with its violet and white flowers for most of the summer. It is easy to protect over winter, but no protection is needed for the little yellow *V. biflora*, which, with the pink *V. rupestris rosea*, will come from self-sown seeds. There are many cultivars in existence to add color, if need be, such as the rich red 'Arkwright's Ruby', the apricot-yellow 'Chantreyland' and the soft pink 'Haslemere'. These will come fairly true from seed as replacements for plants which soon exhaust themselves by flowering. Others, especially those related to the once popular *V. gracilis*, suffer from a virus which has almost

eliminated stocks. Otherwise, the cultivars mentioned above benefit from rejuvenation from basal cuttings or division every two or three years, best in early autumn.

Waldsteinia
(Rosaceae)

This splendid carpeting trailer, *W. ternata (trifolia)*, makes only a brief display of its bright yellow flowers in spring but is excellent as a groundcover in sun or shade, especially over walls. The leaves are of 'strawberry' form, glossy and rich green, giving complete cover. It can be planted at almost any time when not in flower.

Viola cucullata

Viola labradorica

Wulfenia
(Scrophulariaceae)

These form neat tufts or mats of leathery leaves, light green in *W. carinthiaca*. Plants have short spikes of closeset, deep blue flowers 5 in. tall in June and July. An easy to grow plant not objecting to some shade. The smaller, rarer *W. amherstiana* has small, deep green slow-growing mats and arching sprays of lavender blue June to August. It prefers some shade and is only 3 in. high. Division is best in early spring.

Waldsteinia ternata

Zauschneria cana

Zauschneria ○
(Onagraceae)

Although needing winter protection in cold areas these are valuable late flowering plants which are easy to protect. They prefer light, well drained soil in full sun and a southerly aspect. The twiggy growth, with small soft foliage, produces spikes of brilliant scarlet red from August to October. A vigorous plant named 'Glasnevin' is hardier than the grey-leaved *Z. californica, mexicana* and *cana (microphylla)*. All reach 12 in. in height. *Z. canescens* is also grey leaved and any of them will add a splash of brightness when garden color is dwindling. They are increased from cuttings or careful division in spring. They show up well with *Aster thompsonii* 'Nana' and *spectabilis*.

A small section of the classic rock garden using limestone. The yellow sedum is Sedum spathulifolium below a white dianthus, at its best in June.
Below, a prostrate juniper is in need of pruning before it covers another sedum, S. a. murale with reddish foliage.

Alpine bulbs

Very few bulbs have been included in the general list. This is not to say that no others could be recommended, but is more of an indication of the need for discretion. Most alpine bulbs are small in size and difficult to find when dormant, and after introduction they may prove to be unsuitable, too tall, of too rapid a spread, or after flowering they may leave a bare patch. Such risks are inherent, especially as they are often an unknown quantity until tried out for a year or two. Another factor of which account should be taken is that the majority of both alpine plants and bulbs flower in spring — March to June. Even if some bulbs are complementary to the plants flowering at much the same time, one is apt to find a rock garden or bed becomes rather bare of color after June. Where bulbs can be relied upon to come through an over-planting of low carpeting alpines, such as thymes, then nothing is lost, and something is gained, by having two occupants sharing one patch of ground. In view of this the best general recommendation which can be made for those to whom bulbs appeal and who have a site, in particular, where they can be underplanted, is to make a further study of possibilities from specialized books and by observation. Such bulbs as common snowdrop and winter aconite should certainly be excluded and although some anemones with the ability to spread and naturalize have been mentioned in the main list, a warning has been given. There are many noninvasive dwarf bulbs to choose from should one wish to grow some, but this does not rule out the need for discretion.

A rock garden on conventional lines with a good assortment of flowering plants and conifers.

Dwarf shrubs

A few alpines of a shrubby nature have already been included in the general list. There is no strict dividing line, but in the following list each plant has hard wood growth above ground. The emphasis must be on dwarfness because whatever is planted which will grow disproportionately large, will defeat the purpose for which it is used. Shrubs not only add to the display of alpine plants, but give a rock garden or alpine bed a more natural appearance. Shrubs, including dwarf conifers, have shapes and habits different to alpine plants, and as a result of most of them being taller all the year round, will break up any tendency to flatness or uniformity, especially where rocks are not extensively used. The heights given in the following list are those to which they can be expected to grow, followed in parenthesis by the expected spread. These figures can only be approximate or estimated, as with virtually all one grows, height and spread may vary with fertilizer and climate. Some may be pruned, however, to keep them within bounds.

Andromeda
(Ericaceae)

A. polifolia 'Compacta' is a dainty little shrub for peaty, acidic soil, and requires some shade. It makes neat, evergreen bushes 10 in. or so high (8 in. spread) on which hang pearl-like pink flowers in May and June.

Azalea
See under Rhododendron

Berberis
(Berberidaceae)

These are mainly evergreen and prickly. *B. x stenophylla* 'Corallina Compacta' has very small, dark green leaves and clustered flowers of deep orange in May to June, 30 in. (12 in.). A fault in some soils is suckers causing trouble. *B. thunbergii* 'Atropurpurea Nana' grows very bushily 20-24 in. (14 in.), with good purple foliage all the year and orange-yellow flowers in spring. It can be pruned if need be, and is excellent in contrast with yellow cytisus and alyssum. There is a less vigorous, golden-leaved variation in *B. t.* 'Aurea' and two cultivars of note. 'Kobold' is deciduous, with bright greenery all summer and good autumn color, growing to 24 in. (14 in.).

Berberis thunbergii 'Atropurpurea Na[na]'

Cotoneaster
(Rosaceae)

The ground-hugging kinds are effective on rocks or a wall, and excessive growth can be pruned. *C. congestus* has tiny leaves, small white flowers and red berries at ground level and there is a variegated form of *C. dammeri*, more leafy and a little larger. *C. microphylla* has low prostrate growth and this, too, has a variegated form.

Andromeda

Cotoneaster congestus

Cytisus
(Leguminoseae)

These brooms make a splendid display in spring and early summer. They will flourish in poor or dry soil. *C. ardoinii* is only 6-8 in. tall (14 in.) and bears yellow flowers in May. *C. x beanii* is semi-prostrate 16 in. tall (24 in.) with bright yellow flowers in May. *C. x kewensis* is an old favorite, smothering itself in creamy-white flowers, over semi-prostrate growth 6-8 in. high (20 in.). For a large site a spectacular focal point may be created by using the 32 in. 'Gold Spear', a fine sight in May and June with an erect but graceful habit.

Cytisus x kewensis

Daphne cneorum

Daphne
(Thymelaeceae)

These are among the aristocrats in shrubs but are not always easy to suit. In general they like sun and well drained soil. All have heads of perfumed waxy flowers. They grow as mainly erect evergreen bushes from 4 in. to 24 in. in height, flowering in spring and early summer. Species in cultivation include *D. arbuscula*, 6 in., rosy pink, *D. cneorum*, pink, 8 in., *D. collina*, pale lilac, 16 in., *D. retusa*, 16 in., purplish pink and *tangutica*, 14 in., white, tinged purple. Daphnes are rather slow to grow and some do not flower freely until mature.

Erica
(Ericaceae)

The heaths and heathers pose a problem when considering them in conjunction with alpines. Whenever possible they should have a bed to themselves, perhaps with shrubs and conifers here and there, for they have some special requirements regarding soil. In the case of the *carnea* varieties, which do not object to some lime, these spread too widely and engulf smaller-growing alpines. Nowadays there is a vast selection available from specialists, only a few of which would be really suitable as complementary to alpines. These are mostly the lime-hating kinds. In refraining from making specific recommendations it is for the reason that those to whom heathers appeal should consult a book or catalog before making a decision. The best known heathers come under the headings of *Erica*, *Calluna*, *Cassiope* and *Daboecia*.

Erica

Euonymus
(Celastraceae)

The introduction of several new cultivars of these colorful evergreen shrubs has been a stimulant to their popularity. Flowering can be discounted but leaf colors vary from green to gold, purple, silver, etc., and heights range from a mere 2 in. to 20 in. They can be pruned safely in spring to retain shape and have no invasive spread. A selection would best be made on sight, since there are now up to twenty varieties being grown.

Euonymus

Fuchsia and Genista
See main list

Gaultheria procumbens

Gaultheria
(Ericaceae)

These are peat loving and lime hating. The best known is *G. procumbens*, the partridge berry, making carpets of dense foliage, in which nestle the red berries for a long time. It is only 6 in. high but capable of spreading widely where happy. The cultivar named 'Darthuizer' has a more upright growth, larger leaves and berries, and grows 8 in. tall.

Hebe 'Carl Teschner'

Potentilla
(Rosaceae)

P. fruticosa—justification for including these comes from the color they provide in late summer and because they can be pruned back to keep them from becoming too large. Some are too large, but dwarfer growing kinds could include such semi-prostrate species as *P. f. mandschurica*, white flowered, at 16 in. high (24 in.). *P.* 'Elizabeth' *(arbuscula)* may go up to 30 in. (32 in.) if left alone. It is a long flowering light yellow and 'Goldfinger' of similar height is deep yellow. 'Sunset' and 'Tangerine' are both deep orange, but liable to fade in hot sun, as is the otherwise startling 'Red Ace'. This reaches 24-30 in. but with a spread wider than this. Ordinarily, the flowers—as with some others above, extend from early June till autumn—are mostly of a glowing flame-red color. Salmon pink is now seen in *P. f.* 'Royal Flush'. Pruning is best done in early spring.

Helichrysum
See main list

Potentilla 'Sunset'

Hebe
(Scrophulariaceae)

These were formerly included under *Veronica* and are now seen in a much larger variety. They still, however, differ widely in height and form, from such as the minute *H. buchananii* at only 2 in. as a little bush best in a trough or scree, to the shapely green *H. vernicosa*, over 24 in. tall. Many are attractive for their foliage alone, seen in shades of green or of golden hue and sometimes a variegation of these. Other free-flowering kinds such as the popular 'Carl Teschner' with lavender-purple flowers, or white as in *H. brachysiphon (traversii)* are dual purpose. Since so many species and named cultivars are now offered it is probably best to make a visual selection, and to note most are not hardy in cold regions.

Rhododendron
(Ericaceae)

This genus, together with *Azalea*, is best covered by a few general remarks. It is fairly well known that they both prefer lime-free peaty or leafy soil which is neither dry nor fully exposed. There is quite a wide range of rhododendrons and some azaleas especially suitable for rock gardens, but it is likely that very few readers will have the means or situation in which to grow them. Those tempted to do so should first consider the cost in relation to the risks and bear in mind that gorgeous though some are, their period of glory is rather brief and that most of them coincide with the April to June period when the majority of alpines flower.

Rhododendron 'Scarlet Wonder'

A group of miniature roses.

Rosa
(Rosaceae)

Purists would say that the miniature roses are out of place in a rock garden, but there is no valid reason for excluding them if they appeal. They are dwarf, of neat habit, long flowering and colorful. They need pruning a little in spring, not cut back hard, and they need no special soil. A considerable number of cultivars is offered nowadays in pink, white, yellow and red, mostly double. One of the most charming is the parental species *R. pumila* with pink flowers on erect bushes to 16 in. or the double red *R.* 'Oakington Ruby'. Both are very long lived, a virtue not preserved by some more modern cultivars.

Salix
(Salicaceae)

The willows include a few species sufficiently dwarf, but not rated too highly for decorative value. Outward spread is liable to affect surrounding plants, but some have silver leaves and may produce catkins in spring. *S. helvetica* will grow to 24 in. tall (36 in.). *S. lanata* 'Stuartii' is less of a spreader and *S. reticulata* with veined, olive-green leaves is slow growing, good in peat and ground hugging. *S. retusa* 'Pygmaea' makes congested little bushes with greyish leaves 12 in. tall (12 in.).

Santolina
(Compositae)

Only one lavender cotton is really suitable. It is the true dwarf form of *S. incana (chamaecyparissus)* making a year round hummock of grey, like a rounded juniper, with a few yellow buttons in summer. It grows to no more than 8 in. with a similar spread and prefers a dry sunny position. There is now a really dwarf form available called *S. incana* 'Nana'.

Salix lanata 'Stuartii'

Spiraea x bumalda 'Anthony Waterer'

Spiraea
(Rosaceae)

S. bullata is very compact and well clothed with small, dark green leaves. The flower heads in deep pink are freely provided but for only a few weeks, June to August. Height is 12-16 in., (12 in.). The well known *S. x bumalda* 'Anthony Waterer' is too large to consider, but there is a much smaller and more shapely one worth having. It is *S. x b.* 'Nana' or 'Nyewood'. It has heads of glistening pink for many weeks from June onwards. The bushes grow to about 16 in. with as much spread, but pruning does no harm.

A flourishing planting scheme on a wall. Aubrieta, alyssum and alpine phlox grow in crevices between the stones, flowering profusely from April to June.

Plants for special purposes

It should be noted that where a whole genus is named, it does not mean that all members of it are suitable for a given purpose.

Readers should, therefore, refer also to the main descriptive list before making a selection.

For troughs, sinks or scree beds in sun

Androsace, most kinds
Antennaria, dwarfest kinds
Aquilegia, dwarfest kinds
Arabis, slow growing kinds
Armeria caespitosa
Asperula, slow growing kinds
Campanula, smallest non-spreading
Dianthus, smallest kinds
Douglasia
Draba, most kinds
Edraianthus
Erodium, smallest kinds
Gentiana verna and **saxosa**
Geranium, smallest kinds
Globularia, smallest kinds
Hypericum, smallest kinds
Iberis saxatilis
Micromeria corsica
Morisia hypogaea
Myosotis rupicola
Penstemon, dwarfest kinds
Phlox douglasii, some kinds
Polygala calcarea
Potentilla, dwarfest kinds
Primula, only a few suitable
Raoulia, slowest growing kinds
Saponaria 'Bressingham'
Saxifraga, slow growing kinds (Kabschia and Aizoon sections)
Sempervivum, small growing
Teucrium subspinosum
Townsendia formosana
Tunica saxifraga, double flowered

Part of the rock garden at Froyle Mill, Hampshire, England, showing a wide range of plants carefully sited.

Plants for sunny retaining walls and banks

Acaena, most kinds
Achillea, some kinds
Aethionema, most kinds
Alyssum, most kinds
Arabis, most kinds
Arenaria montana 'Grandiflora'
Armeria, some kinds
Aubrieta
Campanula, some kinds
Cheiranthus
Cytisus x kewensis
Dianthus

Erinus
Erysimum
Euphorbia myrsinites
Genista lydia
Gypsophila, dwarf kinds
Helianthemum
Hypericum, most kinds
Iberis
Juniperus, prostrate growing kinds
Lithospermum, some kinds
Oenothera missouriensis
Onosma

Origanum, some kinds
Penstemon, some kinds
Phlox subulata
Polygonum vaccinifolium
Ramonda myconi, for shade
Saponaria ocymoides
Saxifraga, some kinds
Sedum, most kinds
Sempervivum
Thymus, most kinds
Veronica, prostrate kinds

Plants for groundcover between shrubs and in shady places

Acaena in variety
Acorus gramineus
Alchemilla, dwarfest kinds
Ajuga
Arum, some kinds
Asarum europaeum
Campanula, a few kinds
Geranium, some kinds
Gunnera magellanica

Hedera, (ivy), some kinds
Lamium
Liriope
Lysimachia, creeping kinds
Mitella
Ophiopogon
Ourisia
Polygonum affine

Saxifraga, 'mossy' kinds
Sedum spurium
Tellima
Tiarella
Tolmiea
Smilacina stellata
Vinca, (periwinkle)
Waldsteinia ternata

Plants for hot, dry positions in full sun

Acaena, most kinds
Alyssum
Aubrieta
Cheiranthus
Cistus, shrubby
Dianthus, most kinds
Erinus
Erodium

Erysimum
Genista, shrubby
Helianthemum
Helichrysum, most kinds
Hieraceum, dwarf kinds
Hypericum, dwarf kinds
Iberis
Lavandula, dwarf kinds

Penstemon, some kinds
Santolina, shrubby
Sedum, most kinds
Sempervivum
Thymus
Tunica
Veronica, some kinds

Plants for growing in paving

Acaena
Ajuga
Antennaria
Arenaria balearica
Armeria
Azorella
Campanula, creeping kinds
Cotula

Draba repens
Erinus
Hypsella
Mazus
Mentha
Minuartia
Paronychia
Prunella

Raoulia
Saxifraga, 'mossy' kinds
Sedum, some kinds
Sempervivum, some kinds
Thymus, creeping kinds
Veronica, creeping kinds

A variety of pot grown alpine plants with which to begin a collection

An example of the use of alpine plants on a bank

A selection of plants for a partially shaded rock garden

Some explanation may be necessary to emphasize the differences between various types of shade. It must be said that the dry shade beneath overhanging trees is the most difficult of all to fill with interesting, colorful plants. In nature very little plant life exists beneath such trees as maple, oak, beech, ash, chestnut and others which form a dense canopy above. It is not only the exclusion of light that matters, for the tree roots also inhibit plant growth. In summer the soil will become very dry. In rainy weather, there will be drip from the leaves above but this is not the kind of watering which plants appreciate. 'High shade' is better, and it occurs where trees are widely spaced or have relatively little leaf spread. It could also be termed 'light shade' because shadow from tree foliage prevents strong sunlight over a given area below for only limited periods of the day. Daylight is not excluded and the soil between the tree roots does not dry out so much. In forested country, which is often hilly, there is usually moisture in the soil from winter which moves down the slope for much of the drier summer months and this promotes the humidity which many plants prefer.

Adonis
Andromeda, (shrub)
Azalea, dwarfest evergreen kinds
Astilbe, dwarf kinds
Blechnum, fern and dwarf kinds
Codonopsis in variety
Cyclamen
Daphne, dwarf kinds
Dicentra, dwarfest kinds
Disporum
Dodecatheon
Empetrum, (shrub)
Erythronium
Galax
Gaultheria in variety
Gentiana, autumn flowering
Haberlea
Hepatica
Hylomecon
Iris, small varieties
Kalmia, (shrub)
Meconopsis, most kinds

Mentha requienii
Ophiopogon nigrescens
Orchis, most kinds
Ourisia
Patrinia triloba
Pernettya, (shrub)
Polygala chamaebuxus, shrubby
Polygonatum, dwarfest kinds
Primula, some kinds
Ramonda
Rhododendron, dwarf kinds
Salix, small varieties
Sanguinaria
Saxifraga fortunei kinds
Shortia
Soldanella
Thalictrum, dwarfest kinds
Tricyrtis
Trillium
Uvularia
Vaccinium, shrubby

Shade of the best kind is mostly found on north-facing slopes, but in flatter regions one has to make use of shade provided by the walls of structures.

In general, shaded positions do not dry out rapidly, provided the wide-spreading roots of trees and shrubs are avoided.

Dwarf conifers

Abies, dwarfest kinds
Chamaecyparis, dwarfest kinds
Juniperus, dwarfest kinds

Picea, dwarfest kinds
Thuya, dwarfest kinds

Other dwarf shrubs

Hebe, dwarfest kinds
Genista delphinensis

Part of an extensive planting scheme
at the Royal Horticultural Society's Garden, Wisley, England

Index

127